The
Gift
of
Goodbye

The Gift *of* Goodbye

A Story of Agape Love

Rebecca Whitehead Munn, M.B.A.

SHE WRITES PRESS

Published 2017
Printed in the United States of America
Print ISBN: 978-1-63152-230-7

Library of Congress Control Number: 2017931451

For information, address:
She Writes Press
1563 Solano Ave #546
Berkeley, CA 94707

Cover design © Julie Metz, Ltd./metzdesign.com
Interior design by Tabitha Lahr

She Writes Press is a division of SparkPoint Studio, LLC.

This book is dedicated to my mother, Marjorie Ann Pattison Whitehead, who selflessly gave from her whole heart and enabled me to learn to do the same, through the process of saying goodbye. One of my biggest supporters during this writing process was my sister Susan Whitehead, who passed away unexpectedly as I was finalizing my manuscript. This book is also dedicated to her and her willingness to believe in me and support me.

Author's Note

All of the paintings included in the chapters of this book that are not of purple butterflies are original watercolors by my mother, Marjorie Ann Pattison Whitehead. The painting of the purple butterfly was a hand-painted gift from my good friend Liza, and was painted by her daughter Raleigh. The watercolor painting in the Epilogue was painted by the author.

Contents

Introduction

 I grew up in Houston, Texas, in a big family. My four sisters and I were all close in age, born within an eight-year time frame. My childhood and young adulthood was by turns chaotic and comforting, complex and simple, hurtful and joyful, mainly because of the law of large numbers. As I have grown older and, I hope, wiser, and now as a mother of two teenagers myself, I have adapted and thrived, in large part as a result of my upbringing.

As I examine my expansion into my authentic self through writing this book, I appreciate what an amazing transformation I have undergone, both through courage and by choice. I have transitioned from expecting certain outcomes to finding joy in accepting reality as it is and people as they are, from hiding behind masks to enjoying each day as my true self, and from being afraid of the unknown to practicing daily gratitude for the gray that fills in the edges between the black and white of my life.

As a child, I learned to act in ways designed to please others. Through this process, I created many masks to wear based on the expectations I held for myself and based on the beliefs of others. Each appearance or mask was shaped by the "should" view I carried in my mind about my various roles: a sister, a daughter, a friend, and then, later, a leader at work, a parent. But as I started to question my expectations and the various masks I chose to wear, I was able to see clearly that hiding behind these masks concealed the authentic human I am at my core, and wearing the masks hindered my freedom of expression.

Throughout this writing process, I have reflected on and questioned myself and my own beliefs, what I expect of myself, how I react in situations, and whether I am able to persevere when something turns out differently than I expected or someone changes their response from one I have come to trust. After I learned to question the expectations I had of myself, I started to question my expectations of my loved ones and friends—how each of them would react in different situations, what they would feel or do, and how they would stay true to their word. I learned that as I transitioned through big life changes—such as moving from Texas to California, away from my family, and choosing to get married— my heart began to open and I was able to consciously shift my expectations and joyfully accept life as it is, versus how I thought it was or how I wanted it to be.

Now that I have given myself permission to take off my masks and live each day as my true self, I have chosen to dig deep into my heart and acknowledge my greatest passions and desires. Before that, I felt lost without a rudder, unsure of life, and more fear-based. Now, my friends and family would say my true self is a loyal, practical, courageous, and compassionate mother, friend, and sister. After five decades of life, I am finally comfortable in my own skin, regardless of what others think, and rejoice each day in the authentic me I have become.

My development up to this point is grounded in my exposure to religion and faith-based concepts, starting when I was a young girl. I grew up going to church most Sundays with my family. The first church I remember was First Christian Church, which we attended for only a few years after moving to Houston, when I was two years old, and of which I have two distinct memories: one of my baptism, and one of a memorial service for my maternal grandfather. However, I spent most of my years before college as a member of the First Presbyterian Church, where I attended Sunday school and church service most weeks with my family.

Over the years, I became very involved in the church, as I found it a welcoming and inviting place. I felt like I belonged there. I sang in the youth choir, took snow-skiing trips, and taught a bible study class when I was in eighth grade. At the time, I assumed that everyone who attended church gave it their full attention and focus and had a strong faith, just as I was developing. However, as I entered tenth grade, I started to observe the congregants around me more closely and realized that was not the case.

This eye-opening process led me to a place of starting to question the very faith that had been my foundation, my rock, and my source of stability at the time. I was a strong-willed young lady and a little stubborn. I held rigid beliefs that life was black and white. I started to cut back on how much I was attending regular Sunday church service and began my process of questioning people's motives for attending church. In turn, I began to discover that life has a whole lot of gray that fills in the spaces left between black and white. I realized that each of us is experiencing something different at any given moment in time, something that may not be visible outwardly. I also started to shape my understanding of and belief in grace as a way to acknowledge that each of us is doing the best we can with the tools we have been given.

Over decades, and after surviving two major life transitions merely three years apart—going through a divorce with two small children and losing my mother—I have transitioned to practicing daily gratitude for all that is in my life, especially for the opportunity to wake up and be healthy enough to enjoy each day to its fullest. And I have returned to my spiritual roots, this time more expansively than I experienced my beliefs when I was a teenager. Now, as an adult, I experience gratitude for the strong faith I have in a power greater than myself, and for the many blessings that come with letting go, without fear or question.

I grew up in a home that espoused traditional Midwestern values and a sense of loyalty and commitment. While I was raised in Texas, my parents were both born in Indiana, my mom in La Fontaine and my dad in Anderson. My parents met at an Indiana University (IU) event while my mother was still in school there for her undergraduate degree. She was with another man at the event, someone my father knew from his work as a dormitory guidance counselor. The next day, my father asked this man if he was romantically interested in my mom. When he said no, my dad asked for her phone number. My parents started dating shortly after that, fell in love, and were married after an eight-month courtship.

At the beginning of their marriage, they moved around for my dad's work in university administration. He spent eight years at Texas Tech University, during which time my three oldest sisters were born. In 1960, my parents moved back to Bloomington, Indiana, from Lubbock, Texas, so my dad could return to school at Indiana University. The sister closest to my age and I were both born in Bloomington while my father worked at IU and completed his doctoral degree. All seven of us lived in a two-bedroom apartment during those years, and while space was scarce, I felt love as I came into this world. When I was two years old, my father graduated from IU and accepted a position as associate dean of students at the University of Houston, and we moved to a three-story house just two blocks from the Texas Medical Center and Rice University.

My mother was a quiet leader in her own right. Her goal in raising my sisters and me seemed to be to empower us to believe that we could accomplish anything we desired. She indulged all of our individual passions and yet somehow made me feel as I were the only person who mattered when I spent time with her.

My parents were happily married for fifty-five years. Their marriage ended when my mother passed away at age seventy-seven, when I was forty-three. She was diagnosed with rectal cancer as I was going through a divorce with two young children, ages two and four. Following her diagnosis, she started treatment with traditional Western methods: radiation and chemotherapy, followed by surgery, but she quickly felt in her body that while that regimen was killing the cancer cells, the drugs were also killing her healthy cells. She suffered many of the debilitating side effects of chemotherapy, including mouth sores, diarrhea, and dry eyes. After she had surgery, she was able to withstand only a portion of her chemotherapy treatments. A year and a half later, when she discovered the cancer had metastasized into her lungs, she was determined to have a good quality of life for whatever time she had left. She chose to take Chinese herbs daily and receive weekly acupuncture treatments. She lived fairly comfortably for another year and a half using these Eastern-medicine techniques, in addition to taking daily walks around her neighborhood on Lake Austin.

Mom taught me so very much, both in her fruitful living years and in her last year on Earth. She was a voracious reader, always questioning the status quo and expanding her traditional faith to incorporate more metaphysical beliefs. Even in dying, she gave me an eye-opening and heartfelt opportunity to learn from her views. One important lesson she taught me through the process was that we don't really have to say goodbye to our loved ones as they pass from physical life. Rather, as they transition and take on the form of angels, they remain engaged in our lives by watching over us, cheering us on through our many joys and supporting us through our tribulations. And sometimes, if we are open to believing it is possible, our loved ones boldly make themselves known and forever change our physical lives for the better.

When I watched the 2012 movie *Brave* with my children, memories of me as a stubborn and strong-willed young girl flooded my thoughts, reminding me of how determined I was to make my own path in life without having much of a relationship with my own mother. Although I realize in hindsight how much loving grace and support without boundaries she afforded me when I was a young girl, how many chances she gave me to let her into my life and my heart, I struggled to give her full credit for empowering me at the time. Feeling deep love did not always come easily to me. My sense is that because I was raised by parents who had multiple advanced degrees and who valued intellectual, thought-provoking discussions, I lived from a place of intellectual and mental focus. In this environment, I was always seeking to understand the big picture and why things were the way they were. I felt most comfortable thinking or doing, versus being and feeling.

Now, though, as I watched *Brave* with my own children, I saw the movie as a gentle nudge to remember not just where I came from but also who I had grown to be, all that I had survived and evolved through, and I decided that maybe it was a good time to turn my story into a book.

Then, at church the next morning, our pastor ended his talk with a challenge for all of us "to seek what we were put here to do." He talked about how each of us has special talents and gifts that we are meant to share. He ended by saying, "God loves us. Now what? Go out and do something." Here was another voice speaking to me, nudging me forward. And here I am, venturing into the unknown to share my story of how my heart was able to expand and feel deep love beyond any boundaries my mind was able to imagine.

In the midst of my pain about my divorce and my mother's death, I struggled to understand what love really was and started to question my beliefs. Without my husband or my mother at my side, I felt a gaping void where my heart should have been; as if it had been ripped out of my body and a deep ravine had cut through the middle of my chest in its place. After losing two people I had been so connected to, I wondered how I would survive without either of them.

I stumbled through life in those days almost blindly. Because I inherited the lifelong-learner trait from my mother, I started reading book after book, hoping to find meaning in the word "love." I also experimented with different types of healing therapy, from healing touch to cranial-sacral therapy, to help my body and soul recover.

After many therapeutic experiments and countless books, I finally found a worthwhile definition of "love" in the book *The Gifts of Imperfection*, a birthday gift from my friend Karen. The definition is based on author Brené Brown's thorough research and decades of interviews:

Love: We cultivate love when we allow our most vulnerable and powerful selves to be deeply seen and known, and when we honor the spiritual connection that grows from the offering with trust, respect, kindness, and affection. Love is not something we give or get; it is something that we nurture and grow, a connection that can only be cultivated between two people when it exists within each one of them—we can only love others as much as we love ourselves. Shame, blame, disrespect, betrayal, and the withholding of affection damage the roots from which love grows. Love can only survive these injuries if they are acknowledged, healed, and released.

Belonging: Belonging is the innate human desire to be part of something larger than us. Because this yearning is so primal, we often try to acquire it by fitting in and by seeking approval, which are not only hollow substitutes for belonging, but often barriers to it. Because true belonging only happens when we present our authentic, imperfect selves to the world, our sense of belonging can never be greater than our level of self-acceptance.

Dr. Brown talks about how love and belonging are connected and how our truest self is our most vulnerable and authentic self. Her concepts mirror many of the lessons I have chosen to take away from my heart-opening journey to authenticity. For example, I know now that the many masks I learned to wear were founded on my quest to strive for perfection, in my schoolwork, in my relationships, and, later, in my work life. If only I did more or tried harder, I thought, I would reach perfection. Sadly, that is not a very warm place to be and left me feeling empty. Because of my fierce determination in gripping tightly to the person I thought I was, and because of my stubbornness about not letting go of my ego and trusting my faith, my path to healing was long and circuitous. As I stand here on the other side of these many experiences, some ten years later, I believe that the nature of the process and the choice I ultimately made to expand my faith were what allowed me to achieve authenticity and venture into a more complete and rewarding way of life.

As I questioned my faith in my late teens and early adult years, I grew more afraid of the unknown. I held on tight to my beliefs and to concepts that made me feel safe. Or so I thought at the time. For example, I loved butterflies as a child and went to several butterfly museums when I was growing up. I remember standing in awe in the glass enclosed butterfly rooms as I watched many different kinds of butterflies move about the space, seemingly so effortlessly. I never saw a purple butterfly in any of those museums or in pictures in books, so I used to think purple butterflies were a creative and lovely figment of my imagination but not real in nature.

However, as I deepened my faith and my ability to love with my heart wide open, my perceptions began to shift and I became more open to believing in miracles and things that my mind had not yet comprehended— open to trusting that there was more to life than what I had seen or could see. I learned through experience that if I believed something could be possible, in some cases it was. Purple butterflies were one example. While I had never seen one in nature, I chose to believe they were real. Now, my changing beliefs about them have come to represent the arc of my personal evolution that this book is intended to convey: my heart-opening journey to authenticity, a daily practice of gratitude, and expansive joy.

The more joy we have, the more nearly perfect we

are. My transition from living life from a place of fear to trusting my faith in something greater than myself has opened my eyes to a whole new world. As I have reflected on my experience of living through two major life transitions within a three-year span, I have realized the amazing shift I have made is due to the lasting gift of love from my now-deceased mother, and to my courage, and to the choice I made to expand into more of who I am at my core as everything about life as I knew it changed. My intention in sharing my story is to provide firsthand examples from my own heart-opening expansion that will encourage you to believe that you, too, can form new beliefs and new connections and elevate your experience to a higher level of authenticity. Thank you for reading.

Chapter 1:

Venturing into the Unknown

Do the one thing you think you cannot do.
Fail at it. Try again. Do better the second
time. The only people who never tumble are
those who never mount the high wire. This
is your moment. Own it.
—Oprah Winfrey

My mom came into this world a warrior, weighing in at just four pounds at birth on March 9, 1929. It was a miracle that she lived at all. She was the lone survivor of four children born to her mother and father.

Her brothers and sisters were also very small and died either at birth or shortly thereafter. As a result, Mom grew up an only child, born under the sign of Pisces. In her journal, she captured some key descriptors of her sign: "generous, compassionate, receptive, imaginative, and efficient"—all representative of the mother I came to know as the youngest of her five daughters.

Her mother was on the city council of the Indiana town of six hundred people where she grew up, and her father owned the only gas station and auto-repair garage. My mom described to me how her mother pushed her hard to succeed and even acknowledged sometimes that she was doing things in such a way that my mom would not be spoiled. I never got a chance to know my maternal grandmother, as she died when I was only four, but I imagine she carried such deep pain in her heart from losing three children that it hindered her from having any kind of truly loving relationship with my mom.

Nevertheless, when I was growing up, my mom was always smiling and always seemed calm. She appeared to know all, had a solution to every problem, and seemed to possess every possible skill needed to raise five girls born within an eight-year time span, seemingly effortlessly and with great love. Many people described Mom as Betty Crocker, Donna Reed, and Mother Teresa, without the notoriety, all combined in one person. She could make any occasion seem special, such as when she played the piano at home. I would sit in the green chair behind her and listen as her fingers floated seemingly effortlessly across the keys. The emotion and mood she created as she played sounded as elegant as a concert recital.

Mom had an innate joy and passion for being creative in other ways besides playing the piano. She was always open to engaging in arts-and-crafts projects, including papier-mâché and sewing, and brought her playful self to each endeavor. As an only child herself, Mom wanted her children to have lots of playmates. She was always offering for us to bring friends home from school and planned countless slumber parties. Our home became a destination for our friends, and Mom became a mother of sorts to her many "adopted" daughters. I still laugh every time I think about how our house became known as the Cheese House. Mom would buy cheddar cheese in bulk from the meatpacking plant; it came in a huge half-moon shape that took up half of a shelf in the refrigerator. My friends and I would pull out the cheese after school and cut slices to snack on, then wrap it up and return it to the shelf.

In July 2003, in Boulder, Colorado, I was struggling through a heart-wrenching life transition: a divorce from the father of my four-year-old son and two-year-old daughter. He and I had reached a point of irreconcilable differences, although I never could have predicted that, given how strong our relationship was in its early years.

It was eight years earlier when I had met him, in 1995. I was at work one day when Mike, the guy across the hall from me at work, stopped by to catch up. He was excited to tell me that he had hired a new salesperson, a man from North Carolina, whom he had worked with before. Mike said this new employee went by his middle name, Leslie, and that he was moving out to San Francisco to run the western territory. In addition to sharing what a great person and successful salesman his friend was, Mike mentioned that he thought Leslie and I would enjoy spending time together.

Mike convinced me to be brave and oblige the introduction. I was very nervous and not sure how to handle myself or what to say. It had been a long time since I had been out on a date and I was out of practice. However, my heart had already begun to expand by that time, so I was definitely more open to new experiences than I had been in the past.

The next week, Leslie came to Austin for training. Mike came by my office to get me, and I followed him down to the training room to meet Leslie. I can remember that day like it was yesterday. Leslie was a tall, dark-haired, handsome man with a warm smile. We shook hands, and I felt electricity between us immediately. Although I was uncomfortable showing my interest, since we were at work, I was not able to hold back my emotions entirely. I felt a blush sear my cheeks, and for a minute, I felt as if my face were on fire. I turned my head away, embarrassed, yet I could still feel Leslie looking at me.

Our introduction was short-lived, as he had to go back to training. He said he wanted to talk more and asked for my phone number. He was flying back out to San Francisco later that afternoon. I went back upstairs grinning from ear to ear, excited and full of energy and still feeling the blush on my cheeks. *What just happened?* I asked myself, even as I was already starting to think about what I would say the next time we spoke.

Leslie called the next day. He was getting settled in his new apartment in Sausalito and lived a mile from the San Francisco Bay. As we talked, he told me that he had grown up in Charlotte, North Carolina, and had four siblings. I didn't often meet someone else from a big family like mine; it felt comforting to me and established something familiar between us right away. We started talking on the phone most days, some days for hours, and e-mailed some as well, getting to know each other over several weeks. Every time I talked to him, passion and excitement filled in more space that my fear had once occupied.

Since he was in sales and I was leading our healthcare business unit, Leslie was determined to find healthcare sales opportunities that we could pursue together. He secured some meetings for us in Oakland, and I went out for a visit, where I confirmed my sense that something special was growing between us. I also became comfortable enough with him to take a weekend trip to San Francisco. I planned to stay with my sister who lived there but also intended to spend time with Leslie while I was there.

I loved the outdoors, and Leslie's idea of a first date was hiking in Muir Woods. We walked along under the gentle-giant redwood trees that reached far up into the sky, standing peaceful yet strong in the wind. I felt as if we had escaped to a magical place. We started holding hands as we hiked. After a couple of miles, we stopped to rest on a bench, and then he leaned over and kissed me. The blush spread all the way across my face as I beamed at him. We continued hiking for several hours and then went to dinner, where I started to get sad, as I knew our invigorating time together had to come to an end. We kissed goodbye as he dropped me off at my sister's house.

That night, as I prepared to go to sleep, I decided maybe Mike was right about Leslie and me: unique and lovely feelings for him were indeed growing in my heart. And those feelings appeared to be mutual, as Leslie soon approached me to figure out when we could see each other again.

A month later, we met in San Diego for a business meeting on a Friday morning. We both felt fortunate to have a work excuse to reconnect and spend another weekend together. We spent the day at Sea World and bought matching sweatshirts. Leslie had done his research on romantic places to eat and had made reservations for dinner at the Marine Room in La Jolla. I was surprised and excited that here was someone working hard to win my heart. It had been many, many years since a man had paid so much attention to me.

As we sat and ate dinner, waves crashed up against the window. I felt as if we were the only people in the restaurant as I looked in his eyes. He put his hand on my arm and smiled. His charm and wit swept me away. He also had a great sense of humor, which I loved and which was quite a change from what I had known growing up with an always-serious father. As my heart and my faith in something bigger than myself continued to expand, I felt the joy and playfulness of this love growing between us begin to command my daily focus, more than my fear of my heart getting stomped on did.

The following year, Leslie and I decided that it was better for us to live in the same area for a while before our relationship got more serious, so I moved to San Mateo, California. My sister lived there, too, so I was willing to move near her, on my own, without any expectations. I found a two-bedroom house to rent in San Mateo, and Leslie helped me find a job through some of his work contacts. We each sometimes spent several hours in traffic during the week in order to see each other, since he still lived in Sausalito. Our favorite Saturday-morning date was to ride bikes to downtown San Mateo and eat brunch. He would stay at my house and help take care of my chocolate Lab, Carmella, when I had to travel for work.

Over Labor Day weekend 1996, he proposed to me at the Palace of the Fine Arts in San Francisco, and we were married in 1997. The armor around my heart started to dissolve, inch by inch, with the persistence of my husband's love. An emotional thinker, a passionate dreamer by nature, he acted in a spontaneous way much of the time. He was my opposite in some ways and, at the time, probably a good model for me to encourage the continuing softening of my edges, my heart-opening journey to authenticity.

When we married, I was thirty-three and he was thirty-six. He moved in with me in my house in San Mateo, a modest 1,800-square-foot home with two bedrooms and a small yard for Carmella. We shared many dreams, including wanting to have children. Following a year of working hard and spending several hours commuting to work each day, we sat on our front porch one Friday night and checked in on our dreams. We were both feeling as if life was leading us and all we did was work, and we knew if we wanted to have time for children, we would need to make some changes.

Leslie looked at me and challenged me to a game. We went inside and pulled out a map of the United

States. The game was to pick three states where we would each want to live. The one place we both picked was Colorado. We shared stories of childhood trips we'd each taken there and decided either Denver or Boulder would be a good place for us to live and work.

The very next week, Mike, the guy who introduced us, called Leslie seemingly out of the blue to share some news. He had just accepted a position at a company in Boulder and wanted to hire Leslie to lead his sales-partner program. Leslie and I both sat speechless, looking at each other, after he hung up the phone. Here was our answer—a path to get us where we wanted to go.

Leslie started commuting for work, and we moved to Boulder five months later. As we closed on our new house, I discovered I was pregnant. After that, life seemed to accelerate rapidly. While we continued our date nights, hikes, and golf games, the stress of the many demands of married life seemed to increase. In a few years, we bought our first house, had two children, added onto our house and finished the basement, then bought a second home, in the mountains about an hour away. Leslie was a passionate dreamer and continued to want more, but, after spending my days working and nights taking care of our babies, I was starting to feel disconnected from him, as well as reverting to the people-pleasing patterns I had adopted in my childhood. He would bring up ideas of getting a hot tub for our second home or getting a new car, and I would go along with his dreams.

Our deep love started to become more strained when he was laid off from his job. The company was changing directions and no longer needed his services. It was just after our daughter was born. The incident afforded us some much-needed one-on-one time, as I was also off work, for maternity leave. We spent twenty days before New Year's snow-skiing together as our nanny took care of the children.

After I returned to work in January 2001, Leslie decided he was more of an entrepreneur and wanted a small-company experience. He tried a couple of start-ups, which seemed promising at first, only to fold months later as their funding ran out more quickly than sales could materialize. I took on head-of-household responsibilities as he struggled to find his place. Once again, our full days of taking care of our young children and our two homes sapped our attention, and we started to grow apart. Finally, in the spring of 2003, I felt in my heart after trying to resolve our differences in six months of marriage counseling that it was healthier for everyone for us to part ways.

In the midst of changing almost everything I knew, from my marital status to the type of job I had, I was grateful to have some constants in my life that enabled me to keep going, put one foot in front of the other, and not look back. My mom and dad were some of my strongest supporters.

One day, my dad called and asked what I needed. I'm sure he was expecting me to say money, which he thought could heal any ill. Dad was in charge of the finances in our home when I was a child, and he taught me how to build and manage a budget. He grew up in a very modest household and was the only one of three children in his family to attend college. He was determined to make something of his life and set out on his path in college. Even as he developed his promising university career, he remained a miser. With Mom's help, he was able to stretch a dollar further than what I thought was possible growing up. Through his hard work and some financial blessings, he developed a solid fiscal foundation later in his career. Offering to give me money was his way of giving from his heart.

While I was grateful, what I needed most at this moment in 2003 was for my mom and dad to come help me through the dissolution of my seven-year marriage, be by my side, supporting me daily, wrap my babies in their love, and help us all survive the worst—or at least what I thought was the worst at the time. My dear friend Lyn says God gives us only what we can handle. Back then, a divorce with small children was more than I thought I could handle. However, since my kids were looking to me for guidance, I learned through trial and error how to take each day as it came, face the fear and uncertainty, and carry on. Some moments felt like quicksand, others like water, and every day felt like a wall of grief I had to face. But even though I thought I had all I could handle and that I had experienced the worst loss possible, time would soon show me that my heart would expand to handle more as the depth of my loss widened.

~❧~

My mom and dad came to live with us in Boulder in late July 2003 and helped wherever they were able. It was a trip that had no defined end, and they were committed to staying until I felt stable. Words are not worthy to describe what an incredible gift of the heart it was to have them both by my side, calming me and bringing me peace by being present. In addition to helping with daily chores, Mom and Dad showered my children with acts of loving-kindness, indulging my two and four-year-olds in the whim of the moment, focusing intently on their stories, and playing games until their hearts were content. They were there as my husband and I ventured into mediation sessions about how to split our family and figure out fair parenting schedules. Our mediator helped us determine the parenting arrangement that would support our children best.

One day in August 2003, as my mom was picking up toys around the house, I saw her taking small breaths, kind of like the type of breathing that I learned in birthing classes as I prepared to have my babies. Mom tried to keep it to herself and kept a smile on her face as best she could. I chose not to say anything at first, maybe because I was scared of the answer or maybe because I was too absorbed in my own pain. Day after day went by, and as I started to notice her doing it more and more often, I became increasingly concerned. When I gathered enough courage, I asked if anything was wrong. "Mom, I've been noticing you take little short breaths as you walk around the house. Are you feeling okay?"

Mom sounded scared when she answered, "I'm feeling a little pain. The breathing helps. It's nothing to worry about. I'm sure I just pulled a muscle or something."

At the time, I was so distracted by my own suffering that I dismissed her symptoms as nothing. Then, one day we were hiking in the open space near my house and she opened up a little more about the quick breaths she was practicing. Mom had never complained once a day in her life. Even when she went through chemotherapy and radiation for late-stage breast cancer when I was in college. Even when she endured bone marrow and liver tests every six months for fifteen years to make sure her breast cancer had not spread. She had gone to those tests every six months very quietly, relying on close friends for support and never talking to my sisters and me about how it felt. I didn't learn until much later how painful those tests she endured were for her. That was the toughness my mom had represented to me in the past; she had always seemed like someone who could withstand anything. What she shared at that moment on the trail, though, told me this was a whole lot more than nothing. Mom was experiencing some bleeding and having lower-hip pain, a feeling of pressure near her tailbone.

As we talked more, I learned that a year and a half before, her colonoscopy had revealed a small, benign polyp that she had subsequently gotten removed. Her doctor had recommended another test in three years, thought she had nothing to worry about, or so he said at the time. His recommendation was based merely on clinical guidelines for follow-up on normal cases.

I realized then that Mom had chosen to ignore her pain and bleeding and had not gone to see her doctor before she and my dad had come to live with me. I wondered if this was connected at all to her previous colonoscopy. My sense was that something was definitely wrong, although my ability to process anything beyond daily coping remained quite difficult for me at the time.

Still, my heart grew heavier each day with the knowledge that Mom was helping me while she suffered inside. That was my mother, always giving to others, always selfless. One day, as I packed and prepared to move to my new home, my eyes welled up with tears. I was frozen in my tracks as thoughts of my changing reality popped into my head. I struggled with understanding how another life transition could be starting to take shape, one even more life-altering than a divorce. *Oh, no, God, I am not ready*, I thought. *I am not strong enough.*

~❧~

On August 28, 2003, I felt my wall of grief hitting me the hardest. Everything I knew about my identity—my home, my job, and my marriage—was proceeding to an end. As I continued to grapple with the amount of change I was processing, I felt like a child in some respects and like I was expected to be the Rock of Gibraltar for my own children in other ways. I started each day feeling as if I were facing a mountain I was not able to climb and ended with breathing a sigh of relief that I had made it through.

Supported by and armed with the unconditional love of my parents, my children and I made it through the start of school and the move to our new home. I felt freer being in a new place—a place free of the pain and loss my divorce represented; a place where I could create new memories and decorate in a new way. Several weeks later, I finally convinced my mom that I was stable enough that she could go home and see her doctor. She agreed, and soon after that, she and Dad returned to Austin, where she was able to get in to see her doctor quickly. He ran several tests and told her to await the results.

Even as I transitioned to making new memories in my own family—creating a new place called home, unpacking box by box—and as my children were experiencing new adventures, such as climbing the three-story oak tree in our front yard, I grew more and more concerned about Mom. I couldn't help but feel in my heart that something very sad was unfolding for her.

And then the news came. In early October, my sisters and I were all stunned when Mom's test results came back. The tests showed an ulcer-like, malignant tumor the size of a grapefruit in the lower part of her colon. She had a fast-growing, atypical kind of cancer. I felt my face flush and my stomach turn inside out as my body swelled and seized up with anger, shock, and fear of the unknown. I couldn't process even the concept of losing my mom—she and I had worked diligently to forge a strong and meaningful bond over the previous ten years. I treasured and cherished our growing relationship. And here I was, facing the reality of life once again tapping me on the shoulder and asking me to be strong, handle another difficult situation. The little girl inside me screamed at the awful timing of this news. I was sure I was not strong enough to endure more loss, especially that of my mom, who was the one constant who gave me strength.

My warrior mom was not a novice to cancer. She had faced the challenge once already, when I was in college. During my junior year, the phone rang one Thursday night. I can still remember the moment as if it happened yesterday. I was lying on my bed, studying for a marketing test. I answered the phone and was happy to hear my mom's voice on the other end. I thought she would say hello quickly, as she had done many times before, and check in on my schoolwork, but as she started to speak, her words filled me with fear.

Mom said, "Rebecca, I'm calling to let you know that I saw the doctor today. I was having some pain trying to raise my right arm. The appointment happened so fast, and he ran a bunch of tests. I was there all day and am exhausted. I need to tell you that I have been diagnosed with late-stage breast cancer."

I was speechless as she continued to tell me more, struggling with processing all the details she shared. The tests showed a tumor the size of a grapefruit on top of her right breast. The cancer was fairly advanced, as it had spread to most of the lymph nodes on her right side. Still, she said she was not really having any symptoms. That was my mom—always focusing on everyone else's needs first and not paying attention to her own body.

"My doctor wants to act quickly and has scheduled surgery for tomorrow at Methodist Hospital," she went on. "I would like you and your sisters to come to Houston. I know that will be hard to manage. I'm going to be okay. I love you."

Although I struggled to get words out to respond to the news I had just heard, I managed to tell her how much I loved her and hung up. All night, I tossed and turned, afraid of what might happen next. My heart raced, and chills rolled up and down my spine. As each hour passed, my body became more exhausted while my mind actively thought of what this really meant for me.

I realized at around 2:00 A.M. that I had taken my mother for granted. I had learned to count on her always being there, and this news had caught me totally by surprise. What would happen next? Was Mom really capable of surviving this illness, which sounded very serious? My fear took over my whole body. My palms became sweaty, and my stomach to turned over and over, like waves crashing on a beach. Finally, I instinctively put one hand on my stomach and one hand on my heart and dozed off for a few hours.

The next day, I awoke in what felt like a haze, wondering if it had all been a dream—until I talked to my sister and realized it was real. We discussed our days and determined that we could leave Austin a little after lunch for the two-and-a-half-hour drive to Houston. I then called one of my teachers to let him know about my situation and that I would have to miss my afternoon class. Then my sister and I drove to Houston to be with Mom and planned to stay through the following week.

On that Friday at 5:00 P.M., we arrived at our childhood home, which was just a few blocks from the Texas Medical Center and Methodist Hospital, where Mom had had her surgery earlier that day. Shortly thereafter, we went to the hospital to get an update. The doctor had reported that the procedure had gone well. He had been able to remove the tumor on her right breast. Because of the advanced stage of her cancer, he had also removed seventeen of the eighteen lymph nodes in her right armpit.

Over the next few days, my sisters and I took turns going to visit Mom at Methodist Hospital, where she was staying, recovering from the surgery. Each of us was still in shock about the news and somewhat withdrawn from the reality facing us. While we were all focused on Mom, we also learned how dependent on her our dad had become. On Saturday, while I was at the hospital and one of my sisters was home taking a nap, my father went to wake her up. She was startled and worried something else had happened to Mom, until she learned that he expected her to make his lunch, just as Mom had done day in and day out on the weekends before, taking care of others' needs before her own.

The first day when I went to visit Mom, I remember distinctly that I found her lying in her hospital bed after her radical mastectomy on the right side of her body. She looked exhausted and yet peaceful. Her face lit up when I walked into the room, and energy seemed to flood her body. My heart filled with joy at the opportunity to see that she was indeed okay. I ran over and hugged her as tears rolled down my cheeks. For what seemed like hours, I held on tight, like a little girl afraid of the dark. Finally, I kissed her on the cheek, sat next to her on her bed, and asked her to share what the experience had felt like to her.

Despite the reality that she had learned only a few days earlier of the cancerous tumor and had come through a difficult surgery, Mom was determined to focus quickly on her healing. She surprised me with her first request. She asked that I help her healing process. She wanted to teach me something about visualizing her body being healed. Although that concept was quite confusing and foreign to me at the time, it was typical of my mom to want to move forward and focus on the positive, despite her circumstances. I also knew how strongly she believed in the power of her mind and its capacity for healing her body. So a little voice inside me told me to be open to her request and follow her wishes. Here was a chance for me to give back a little, as she had done countless times for me before.

She said, "Rebecca, I know it is possible for me to survive this cancer. I am much stronger than any disease. The whole time I have been lying here in this hospital bed following my surgery, I have been focusing my attention on healing. And now I want a little of your help."

Mom's conviction in the idea that the mind can heal the body stemmed in part from her study of the book *Love, Medicine, and Miracles,* by Bernie Siegel, and in part from her grandmother Dora Annetta, who had been a healer of sorts. Mom approached her healing from her cancer surgery much as Dora Annetta would have: with persistence and determination.

As I sat there in her hospital room, now a willing participant, Mom instructed me, "Now, focus all of your mind and attention on the affected area up here on my right breast, and imagine the cancer cells evaporating like water on a hot, sunny day."

I closed my eyes and tried to visualize exactly what she asked. We sat there for what felt like hours with our eyes closed, trying to keep our attention focused on picturing the cancer dissolving. As I practiced this new skill, my mind wandered a bit. I thought about things that dissolve or fade away in nature. I loved welcoming the spring flowers after the frozen hibernation of the ground in winter. One of my favorite things to do as a little girl was to pick a stem of goat's beard wildflowers with the seed head still intact. I would hold a bloom in my hand, close my eyes, and make a wish, then open my eyes and blow the white seeds away. Each stem would disappear one at a time, carried off by the wind.

As I thought of this experience, I decided that would be another way for me to visualize Mom's body healing. So I sat there in silence, holding her hand, and, keeping my eyes closed, I imagined the cancer cells being those seed stems. I made a wish for healing then blew the seeds away, imagining the wind taking them to a faraway place outside Mom's body. It calmed my heart to be doing my part in assisting Mom's healing, and she was calmed by my willingness to participate, learn, and help her survive. Day after day, even after she was released from the hospital post surgery, Mom sustained her focus on healing her body on her own and with my help.

After I went back to Austin to resume my college classes, I thought of her each night before I went to bed, and I continued to practice these visualizations. While Mom endured chemotherapy and radiation weekly for the next six months, she suffered many of the common side effects, including hair loss, swollen ankles, and an upset stomach. While wigs are very common today, and organizations like Locks of Love enable healthy people to donate hair for wigs, they were very hard to find in 1984. We were fortunate to live in Houston, where Mom had access to wigs through MD Anderson Cancer Center. She also reached out to her friends to support her and help her process the physical impacts of the cancer. She started taking daily walks with them around her neighborhood and around Rice University's campus, near her house. Her friends provided a safe place for

Mom to release her anger and sadness about the cancer and the changes she experienced in her body. Her face always lit up when she talked about those walks and how much her friends buoyed her. In doing so, Mom modeled for me how valuable ongoing encouragement and love from close friends is to lifelong health.

Around the time I graduated from college, Mom successfully completed her chemotherapy and radiation treatments and moved into remission with grace and reverence. Her hair grew back gray and wavy—a big change from the coal-black, straight hair we had known growing up. Since the cancer was late stage and had spread to so many of her lymph nodes, the medical protocol was to check her body regularly to make sure it did not show up again. So, for fifteen years following the official start of her remission, Mom endured painful bone marrow and liver tests every six months. She would go off quietly to those appointments, without ever drawing attention to the experience or the process. She was so very strong and determined to live a long life and share it with the people she loved.

At the time of her surgery, Mom's doctor had shared with her the appropriate amount of information about her tumor: where it was and what kind of operation he would perform, including removing nearly all of the lymph nodes under her right arm. However, he had stopped short of telling her the odds of her surviving, and at the time I had been so overwhelmed with the shock of what was happening that I had not thought to ask. When I reflected on it later, my interpretation was that he must have believed her situation was tenuous enough, amid all the surgery and treatments, that giving her odds of surviving would not have added anything positive to her outlook or her healing process.

What he did explain to all of us was how advanced a level her cancer had reached, and that it had a 98 percent chance of recurrence. He also mentioned that because Mom's own mother had died of breast cancer, each of Mom's five daughters had a 75 percent chance of getting breast cancer ourselves.

Now, in October 2003, as I sat in my home back in Boulder, I was paralyzed once again, processing the news of Mom's rectal-cancer tests. Her description of the results indicated to me that the clinical prognosis was not good, so I asked for copies of the tests so I could do more research on my own. From reading Mom's PET scan results and through online searches for the clinical research outcomes of similar cancers, I learned what the likely outcome was for someone with her pathology: over a five-year period, the chance of survival for patients who could withstand the entire recommended treatment pre- and post surgery was less than 12 percent. This time, Mom's cancer had spread to her lymph nodes that were connected to all her major organs. When she had survived late-stage cancer before, at age fifty-four, she had proven her determination to fight the disease and heal on her terms. She definitely still had her strong will and was as determined as ever, but now she was twenty years older. I was deeply sad for her, for me, for my children.

As the fog started to clear and my depression surrounding the transition I was living through started to subside, I consciously shifted my focus toward Mom. As I sat quietly in this moment and closed my eyes, I heard a voice and saw a visual of her in my mind. Call it a dream or a gut-level thought, but the message that popped up in my head was: *Mom is not going to survive this time. This is the beginning of the end of her life.*

I attempted to dismiss the thought and tried to focus on something positive, such as imagining her surviving, as she had done so bravely before. But the feeling only grew stronger. My heart began racing, and I let out a gut-wrenching cry, as I thought, *No, God, I am* really *not ready for this. I am not strong enough.*

The combination of this message, Mom's age, and the statistics for people with her health condition made me believe that Mom's body was speaking loudly this time around—something I would come to learn more about over the next few years. Mom's spirit seemed different as well, as if being seventy-four made this time harder and my warrior mom was worn out.

Although I had been in my new home for less than two weeks and was not fully unpacked yet, Mom kept popping into my mind as I carried out my daily activities. My own drama seemed insignificant compared with her news. In the midst of my chaotic life, I knew she needed me, so I called her and offered to go to Austin to be with her.

We talked for a while. Mom seemed somewhat detached and said she was "fine"—that terrible word that often means things are not good. She listened to my offer to come visit and was grateful for the call, but she said I did not need to come now and that it would be better to save the trip for later. Her response gave me pause as I hung up, and I wondered if she was actively feeling her new reality as it unfolded or if she was still trying to make sense of all the new information about the situation she was now facing.

The next morning, the phone rang. It was Mom. She said, "Rebecca, I know you're really busy, but I've been thinking about your offer to come visit. I know I haven't been very good at letting others help me, but are you still willing to make the trip to Austin? I would really like that."

Delighted that she was finally asking for help, I responded, "Of course, Mom. Let me work out the details, and then I'll call you back to let you know when I'll be arriving." I rearranged my schedule, bought a plane ticket, and flew to Austin for the weekend.

When I arrived, Mom seemed very matter-of-fact about her circumstances, claiming that she was not afraid or sad and that she didn't need to cry. Later that day, we went for a walk in the rain. It sprinkled on us as we walked, cleansing and healing us, as we talked about what she was feeling and facing next. All of a sudden, we both jumped and stopped in our tracks as a bolt of lightning struck very close to where we were walking and loud thunder reverberated among the trees nearby. Mom said that was good—lightning brought oxygen, and her body needed oxygen to fight the cancer cells. I smiled. There she was again, twenty years later, focusing on healing her body.

When we got back from the walk, my sisters and I took Mom to the local mall to get a makeover. All the time she spent helping others meant that she rarely made time to put makeup on herself, so we thought taking her somewhere to have someone else focus intently on her would be a nice change for her, and that a little pampering would help her to recognize the beauty we all saw in her.

Mom sat willingly in the chair and waited patiently as the makeup artist went to work, and she made us all laugh when she let the woman know that she did not wear very much makeup and did not want her face caked in it. The makeup consultant started with a very light foundation and some powder to smooth out Mom's complexion. She applied mascara and rose-colored eye shadow to make Mom's eyes come alive, then added blush to further define the beautiful details of Mom's loving face. The woman smiled as she handed Mom a mirror. Oh, how Mom's faced glowed with pure light, her heart exuding joy, when she saw the results reflected back at her.

Despite her newly diagnosed condition, my warrior mom was still able to give and share as she always had. During that visit in Austin, our deep and loving relationship continued to expand. At one point, she starting talking about the latest watercolor painting she was working on and wanted to share it with me. We went to look at the painting, and as I held the paper, I could tell there was more artwork on the back. I turned it over and asked, "Mom, what is *this* painting?"

She chuckled a little and said, "Oh, that wasn't very good, so I started over."

As I looked at the original painting, I disagreed. "Mom," I said, "you are a gifted artist. This painting is amazing. If only you could see the beauty I see. You're being too hard on yourself."

Mom just grinned and brushed off my comment, as she had a hard time receiving compliments, but overall, one experience at a time, I knew she was opening up and sharing more pieces of her life, her joy with me, letting me in. And as she did so, I felt the warmth in my own heart growing. When she needed it most, I was grateful to have a chance to start giving more to Mom from my heart—something that had historically been hard for me to do, as I did not have a great deal of practice in that regard and, through my experiences growing up, had built a protective armor around my heart.

As I reflect on why that was, I think my fear of the unknown was what caused me to build those walls. Because I was a strong-willed girl and a black-and-white thinker, every time I had an experience that revealed something different than what I expected, fear grew in my soul. Over time, I chose to keep my heart protected, as I thought doing so would lessen disappointment. My logical mind believed my heart was safe and no one could stomp on it with this armor. Now, many years later, in this moment of grief about my divorce and pain about the news that Mom was sick again, I could feel how opening up through sharing experiences with her and supporting her from my heart felt safe. Little by little, I began to give from this deep place of gratitude and love.

Chapter 2:

Invincible Me

It has long since come to my attention that people of accomplishment rarely sat back and let things happen to them. They went out and happened to things.
—Leonardo da Vinci

Growing up in a family of five girls was definitely full of drama at times, especially since we shared one bathroom. Despite the challenges and the tension inherent in raising five daughters, Mom managed to encourage and indulge each of our individual interests, from piano lessons to art classes to sports.

When I was in high school, I loved to sing and had been in the choir for a while. I was talking with my mom about an upcoming play at our church and told her I was interested in trying out—but I just didn't think I was good enough to get a singing part. She said, "Rebecca, I hear you singing in your room sometimes, and your voice is strong. I think you're capable of getting a singing part in the church play. I may be biased, I know, but I think you should try. If you don't try, you will never know."

From then on, I practiced day in and day out. Her positive reinforcement and belief in my capabilities led me to give my all during the audition, and it paid off. I landed an important singing role in the play. It felt so liberating to trust myself enough to try something that seemed out of reach and so rewarding when the result turned out in my favor.

I took to heart Mom's positive belief in my capabilities as I became a young woman. I was confident that I could succeed at anything I wanted to, if only I tried. Add my strong will and stubbornness to that confidence in my success, and there I was. Born at the cusp of the astrology signs Aries and Taurus, I came into this world as a "force to be reckoned with," a natural-born leader with a mix of impulsive energy pushing me forward to accomplish my goals and practical energy to help me make sure I worked through the details. Even my name, Rebecca, from the Hebrew word meaning "bound," supported the idea that I would succeed in life.

I went to college to get an accounting degree and

become a lawyer, something I felt compelled to do to please my father. Once at college, I quickly learned that the accounting field was not of interest to me after I struggled through my first class in that subject, so, toward the end of my second year, I changed my major to marketing. The intrigue of the business side of marketing, coupled with my passion for designing dresses growing up, led me to yet another new major: retail buying. My timing for this passion was not great, however, as the retail industry had slid into an economic depression at that time. Jobs in my desired field were very difficult to find, and I wanted to stay in Texas, near my family.

As such, my career out of college followed a different path than I had planned. I joined Brinker International and completed its management-training program, then moved to Amarillo, Texas, for my first assignment. As the months progressed, I was praised for my skills and my role continued to expand. Five years later, I was living in Northern California, leading management training for the twelve stores as a general manager for one of the highest-volume stores in the United States. I was worn out by the stress of the "always on" restaurant world and decided it was time to change careers. I was just starting to think about what I would do next when my mom called and said, "Rebecca, your father had a scary experience in the hospital today. He had a blood clot that caused extreme pain and bruising in his right leg. I took him to the emergency room. The doctor was quickly able to see the clot on the scan and intervene before it moved up his bloodstream to his brain. Your father is very lucky. I'm so relieved."

She went on to describe more of the details of what caused the blood clot, all tied to his heart disease. Once again, I felt my heartstrings pulling me back to Texas as I processed this news from thousands of miles away.

I took a big risk, quit my job, and moved back to Austin. Mom and Dad were willing to have me live with them while I found a new job. I thought it would be easy to make a change, given that I had a marketing degree, but as I looked for work, I found it was more difficult than I expected to find a company willing to hire me in any type of roles outside the hospitality niche. Fortunately, through some business contacts of my parents, I started volunteering in marketing and membership services for MCC, a government-funded research-and-development consortium, and shortly after I started there, a job as the lead of operations and marketing for a telemedicine research project opened up. While I did not know the healthcare industry or the research subject, I was excited to have made a career transition into a fast-growing segment and was determined to master it quickly.

When I found a house to rent with some friends of friends from school, I started to feel not just in control but on top of the world. I believed that even though my future was uncertain, my mom's unshakeable faith in me from when I was young was part of why I felt so confident that I would succeed.

How soon I would learn otherwise. On New Year's Eve in 1994, I was snow-skiing with my friend Stephanie in Breckenridge, Colorado. Having grown up in Texas, I had only gone a handful of times and had taken only a couple of lessons. I could ski down the mountain okay, taking my time, but not with the prettiest form or with much confidence. That day, the snow was falling hard and I was able to see only a few feet in front of me. Still, we made it to the top of the chairlift and ventured out. As I followed Stephanie, an expert skier, we made our way across the top runs. I saw hundreds of beautiful, snow-covered trees as we skied, and their beauty filled my heart with joy. They also distracted me from what I was supposed to be doing, and soon after, it happened: I was following Stephanie's path on the slope, still barely able to see five feet in front of me, and all of a sudden, I found myself flying through the air, having skied off a jump. Surprisingly and somewhat awkwardly, I landed straight up on both skis. At that, a mixed sense of shock and triumph shot through my veins. I was feeling quite accomplished, as I had never skied off a jump before, and my confidence quickly took over. *This skiing is easy stuff*, I thought. *I can do this!* I anxiously awaited the next challenge, trying to stay close enough to keep the green color of Stephanie's ski jacket in sight.

My goal was to keep going and follow my friend. As the snow continued to fall, the depth of the snow and the difficulty level of each run were hard to discern, but the thrill of skiing down the mountain in areas I had never been to overshadowed the reality of my true abilities.

The next thing I knew, I was knee-deep in a mogul field on a very steep run. I had only been skiing down the bumps for a few turns and then on one turn, my left leg and ski kept turning after cresting the mogul. And then I heard a loud *pop*. Ouch. I felt pain shooting through my leg, and I lost all strength to stand in that moment. I plopped onto the ground and straightened out my leg, which helped the pain subside. After a little rest, I thought I would be able to ski down.

Boy, was I wrong. When I stood back up, I realized I did not have much stability or strength in my left leg. Stephanie had made it back to where I was by that time and quickly called for ski patrol. Soon I was wrapped up tightly on a toboggan, being pulled down the run peppered with the most moguls in Breckenridge. Yes, I was invincible, or so I was used to feeling. Riding down the mountain, staring at the sky above, I realized, *Not so much*.

As the patrolman skied down with me wrapped up in the toboggan behind him, I closed my eyes. It started to sink in that maybe I had limits. I thought about how I lived my life in high gear, always going. This injury was definitely going to slow me down, and I knew I would need to rely on others to help me recover from it. I felt scared and vulnerable, but also, here was an invitation. This was a wake-up call that was valuable not just physically but also psychologically. It represented a turning point for me to start to open my heart.

The ski patrol delivered me to the Breckenridge Medical Center. While the examination yielded a diagnosis of a torn anterior cruciate ligament (ACL), I wondered why I was not able to walk on my leg, as the other patients around me seemed to be able to do without pain. I was soon released with crutches and pain medication, but that evening, I was unable to straighten my left leg. The pain seemed to be getting worse, and my knee continued to swell. I knew I needed another medical opinion. Stephanie started calling her friends in the medical field for help. There was a world-renowned orthopedic group down the highway called the Steadman Hawkins Clinic. She was able to get me an appointment through her connections the next day.

On the following day, we took a trip to the Vail Medical Center. An MRI revealed a torn ACL and a torn meniscus, inhibiting my ability to straighten my leg. After completing the MRI, I went to a doctor's appointment. I was relieved to be in a place that had some of the best specialists in the world. I started to relax a little, knowing I would be given sound medical advice. Although I was thousands of miles away from home, as I talked to the specialist, I found out he went to Vanderbilt University in Nashville with one of my high school classmates. That made me feel even more comfortable, and I relaxed a little more. I think it helped me focus on what the doctor said to me next. He explained that the injury would definitely impact my long-term mobility and surgery was probably my best option, unless I was willing to cut back on my activity significantly and give up snow skiing. Exercise was a valuable stress-relief valve for me, so that was not an option. As such, the specialist recommended that I head back to Austin for the surgery. He was able to find a fellow who had trained in Vail and provided a referral.

While the flight home was exhausting and challenging to maneuver on crutches, I knew waiting to have the surgery until I was home felt safer and more comfortable. I was able to get an appointment in a couple of days and discuss what would happen next with the surgeon. The surgery to repair a torn ACL and meniscus was an outpatient procedure, and I was told I would be released in twenty-three hours. I scheduled the surgery for a few days later. My mom was willing to take me, and that gave me comfort. I was scared at the thought of surgery and still in quite a bit of pain.

After the procedure, I experienced extensive pain and swelling, likely due to the time that passed between the injury and the surgery. The surgeon decided I needed to be admitted to the hospital, instead of going home. I definitely needed help, as my left leg was immobilized for the most part. The independent girl inside me was too proud to ask for help as a young, now single adult, but as the time passed while I was all alone in the hospital room, I became more afraid. The nurses seemed to be either short-staffed or too busy to attend to my needs.

That night, I cried myself to sleep, still hurting and exhausted from the surgery. I awoke in the night in pain, with a pounding headache. It took over thirty minutes for a nurse to bring pain medication. I think I finally fell back to sleep from exhaustion. The next morning, I awoke in my hospital bed and was pleasantly surprised by a visitor—someone who knew me, who could comfort me. There she was at my side, my mom, treating me lovingly, as if I were still a child. Without my having to ask, somehow she knew I needed her. Whether it was maternal instinct or something else, she dropped everything in her life and came to help me and soothe me.

In those few days, I experienced the most selfless kind of love I had ever felt. Mom stayed with me in my hospital room day in and day out, sleeping in a foldout chair all four nights. She attended to my needs, made sure I had pain medicine, and massaged my shoulders to help me relax. She even gave me a sponge bath, as the nurses never seemed to be around and rarely came to check on me. It was at this time in the hospital, receiving Mom's help and attention to my every need, that I was first able to feel my mom's deep love in my heart. She selflessly gave me her time, support, and, most of all, selfless, unconditional love. This experience represented another turning point for me to start to open my heart.

While I am not a believer that God is responsible for bad things happening, I am grateful for the outcome that this accident created. It altered the direction of my life in a positive way. Mom had raised me to believe that good can come from our life experiences if we choose to see the glass as half full. This perspective had served me well so far and taught me that I was able choose my response when "bad" things happened.

This knee injury, subsequent surgery, and experience in the hospital marked the beginning of an ever deeper relationship between Mom and me. Now, here I was, many years older, in October 2003, and it was my time to give to Mom and share my profound love for her, by supporting her in whatever way she needed. How blessed I felt that she wanted me by her side through the days and months that followed her diagnosis. I somehow felt able to do that now. By listening to the voice of my heart, not my head, I started to practice giving my love in a selfless way, just as she had modeled for me.

Mom was in and out of doctors' offices and hospitals over the month of October 2003. Always the obedient patient, she bravely faced radiation and chemotherapy day in and day out, starting on November 3. Mom had twenty-seven radiation treatments and endured che-motherapy six days a week for four weeks—through a fanny pack–like bag that released the chemo slowly over the course of the week. The doctors said her chances of survival would increase dramatically with this approach before surgery, so she agreed. Mom was ever so strong as these chemicals poisoned her body, and she still never complained about how she felt.

After she finished her treatments, she went to a regular dermatology appointment. Just a routine, annual checkup—until her doctor discovered a mole on her back that looked questionable and removed it. The results came in a week later: it was melanoma, prob-ably related to her having worked in the cornfields as a teenager without sun protection. The news gave me pause, as I was not ready to handle one more thing that validated Mom's quickly deteriorating health sta-tus. I got a lump in my throat as I processed this news and tried to accept the reality of more sickness. Mom's body was speaking even more loudly now; it was not just her rectal-cancer prognosis that was saying the end was near. In my heart, I felt as if her body was tired and likely ready to say goodbye, probably worn out from caring for everyone else. It was just as my vision had predicted. As tears streamed down my face, I closed my eyes and prayed.

> *Lord, fill me with peace and wrap me with*
> *love as I face this unknown, the transition*
> *I am not ready for, the biggest of limbos in*
> *my life.*

Chapter 3:

Awakening

We cultivate love when we allow our most
vulnerable and powerful selves to be deeply
seen and known, and when we honor the
spiritual connection that grows from that
offering with trust, respect, kindness, and
affection.
—Brene Brown

For Christmas 2003, as a recently divorced mother of two, I thought being with my family would be as good an option as any. The family activities and conversation in Austin kept me busy and distracted me from my own reality waiting at home. So, just before the holiday, my sisters and our families gathered in Austin to surround Mom with our love and support. Her energy was low, and yet she pushed through each day and was happy to have us all around. Mom was the unifier of our family, always trying to bring us all together and make sure we all got along. She focused intently on each of our needs, as always, and continued to make us feel special and important.

However, we all walked around each day with somewhat forced smiles. We limited our conversations to quick discussions about the weather, what we were eating, and when we were going to help decorate the tree. I felt as if there were a current of electricity running just under the surface of our interactions. None of us seemed interested in bringing up the topic of Mom and her health; we wanted to keep our emotions in check and to try to enjoy some semblance of a holiday celebration. The visit was short, as we were all preparing for what would happen next: Mom's surgery in January.

When I returned home and walked into my house, tears began pouring down my cheeks, as if a dam had broken loose. I had been holding on to my feelings for days and keeping my spirits up while in Austin, but as I walked through my living room step by step, my reality resurfaced in my consciousness, and the depth of my pain was greater than any I had felt before. Heat spread like molten rock across my chest. Here I was, a newly divorced mother, starting over, while my mom's life was at the mercy of the evil "C" for the second time.

In that moment, my awareness was heightened to such an unbearable level that I started to question whether I could take another step. My knees became weak, and I fell onto the sofa. I had heard stories of former classmates or people I had known growing up becoming addicted to alcohol or drugs to mask pain. In that moment, I felt helpless and could empathize with how they might have felt. I could discern what a fine line existed between being in control and losing my way.

I closed my eyes and drifted off for what felt like hours. All of a sudden, I was awakened by my son tugging on my arm. I sat up and held him for a minute. I looked at him and realized that I needed to be strong, push through the pain, and move forward, if not for me, for him and his sister. So, slowly, I carried on each day, creating my new normal. I continued to expand my faith, seek guidance from a therapist, and spend time with good friends to get through it all. I frequently hiked nearby trails, sometimes with neighbors early in the mornings. We would walk three miles around our neighborhood, solve the world's problems, and watch the sun rise.

Mom chose to have her surgery in Houston at Methodist Hospital, just two blocks from where we grew up, on January 19, 2004. We were all there to support her, along with our many family friends from the area. Her doctor recommended that we go out into the hall and see her as she was being taken in the operating room. As we watched her pass us, she looked angelic, as if lit up from the inside. Her smile was peaceful, her cheeks rosy. As they wheeled Mom away, I closed my eyes and imagined God's pristine light surrounding her and filling her body so it would heal, just as she had taught me many years before.

While Mom was in surgery, my dad, my sisters, and I went for a drive by our old house, two blocks away, where we had created many memories together. I was still holding the vision of healing light wrapping Mom with love and was probably distracted from the conversation taking place in the car. As we turned down our old street and pulled up in front of our child-hood home, I saw something spectacular out of the car window. It was a clear day, and the sun was shining brightly, sending rays of light beaming through the pockets in the branches of trees. The light rays were golden at first, but as I turned my head ever so slightly, I saw deep-blue and purple colors in the rays as well. As I moved my head an inch or two to the right or left, all I saw was the golden light on the green leaves. When I moved back, the vivid hues of blue and purple shone brightly again.

In that moment, I believed I was experiencing an opening to somewhere beyond what we knew on Earth. It was not something easily explainable in words, but what I was sure of was the most amazing feeling in my heart, like the activation of an all-encompassing, calm-ing love. In that moment, I realized that experience was just for me—a special gift. I was not willing to share it with any of my sisters in the car, as I was unsure of how they would react. My sisters were distracted, talking about the old house and memories of growing up anyway, so I kept my impressions to myself and rejoined the conversation as if nothing had happened.

Mom's surgery went very well. She was released to a wing that had nurses who specialized in her type of surgery. She received very attentive care and support for her needs from the staff. We each spent one night with her at the hospital, caring for her and enveloping her in love. On day five, the surgeon pronounced her ready to be released, in much less time than most of his patients—but recovering quickly from any illness had always been her norm.

Mom had arranged to stay with longtime friends in the neighborhood after she was released. She had a follow-up appointment with her surgeon in five days and knew she needed to rest so she could continue to heal.

While I knew Mom's journey had more chapters yet to unfold, now it was time for me to focus on being back home as she was being released from the hospital. Six days after her surgery, I traveled back to Colorado to reengage in my life. I had put everything on hold for the past several months while I traveled many times back and forth to be with Mom. My babies needed my love and support, and I needed to concentrate on finding and transitioning to a new job.

As I was going through my divorce, I had asked my manager to transfer me to a role that did not require travel. She had arranged for me to take on a special project she had been wanting to start yet didn't have the time to work on. She asked me to do some research on how best to create a new liaison role between the consulting and sales divisions. She named me as an interim lead while I helped her shape the job requirements and success measures. While I was saddened by having to let go of the consulting role that gave me such joy, the amount of weekly travel was not something I was willing to do, as it would hinder my ability to support my children through this big life change. This new project enabled me to stay home and work remotely. It also allowed me to use my creative mind and gather support from the sales team, an important internal customer.

I was also ready to finish getting settled in our new home, unpack our remaining boxes, and adjust to our new way of living day in and day out. Learning how to handle every daily task on my own while attending to the needs of a five and three-year-old had its ups and downs. There was always more to do than I could conquer in a day. I felt almost like a child myself, each step feeling like something new. I struggled with getting my strong-willed children to follow basic directions, such as putting on a coat because it was snowing outside. They were each trying to find their way and gain control over something, as everything they knew had just shifted, too.

Then, through my son's kindergarten, I learned of a new way of parenting called Love and Logic, a philosophy founded in 1977 by Jim Fay and Foster W. Cline, MD. The concept felt like a gift from my mother at just the right time for me, as the parenting approach centered on a calm response in the midst of chaos, allowing a child to choose between options as simple as "you brush your hair or I will" and "would you like to wear the blue coat or the pink coat?". My mother represented a calm, practical mother to me and I really did not want to force my children to follow my requests by yelling at them, especially now. In the first class, I learned the basic premise of this parenting style. The goal was to provide choices to your children in regard to decisions you were comfortable with their making—choices such as whether to have Goldfish or pretzels for a snack, or whether to wear the red coat or the purple one. Some days the choice was as simple as either my daughter brushed her hair or I did.

I continued to rely on my faith to give me a little more strength each day. In my most trying moments, I was grateful for a saying that empowered me and calmed my heart. I repeated it often on those days: "When you come to the edge of all the light you know and are about to step off into the darkness of the unknown, faith is knowing one of two things will happen—there will be something soft to stand on, or you will be taught how to fly."

⁓❦⁓

As I was settling into my new life in March 2004, the fog of depression that had surrounded me started to dissipate and clarity began to settle in. I had a little more energy to make it through each day. My daily struggles with getting my children to follow my directions started to lessen as I practiced the Love and Logic parenting tenets. I started to hang pictures on the walls and finished unpacking all the boxes in my new home.

My job situation was also becoming clearer. As a single mom of two, the job still required limited travel, but that was a challenging need to fulfill, as I was working for a company based in another state. I relied on business contacts as I considered options and continued to try to establish where I was to work next. Meanwhile, as I continued to develop the structure for the new interim liaison role, my intuition starting speaking loudly, telling me that soon this position would become a corporate job based in San Jose, versus a job that could be carried out remotely, as I had been able to do for almost a year.

I overheard the leaders talking one day about the importance of this new liaison function and how they needed to hire someone permanently to fill it. I had just survived two major life transitions, one of which had more phases that were yet to unfold. In my new status as a single parent, and as the only one I had to rely on to support my family, I knew this liaison role was not a fit for my new reality.

As the days passed, I worked more diligently to have faith that the right role would present itself. My fear was screaming more loudly each day, trying to get my attention. But each time that happened, I paused, closed my eyes, and imagined releasing a handful of balloons into the sky in a symbolic practice of letting go.

And then it happened. I was offered a new role in a new division with the same company, just three days before my interim position came to an end. It was a corporate-services marketing role, something I knew how to do well from my work experience. I had held various marketing positions for over ten years at that point, so the marketing tasks were ones that came easy for me. Here was just what I needed at the time—a job that was not very demanding of my focus or energy and afforded me the grace of space and time to grieve and

heal my broken heart. This was an important validation in my journey to have faith, surrender my needs to
God, and trust that whatever path emerged, it would
unfold just as I needed it to, and just in time. And what
a life-giving experience—it enabled my heart to open
even further and helped me to believe that what mate-
rialized was what was best for me.

Now that my work situation was solid, I was able
to focus more energy on making our new home our
own. I painted the main bathroom, finished hanging
pictures, and completed the basement organization. All
of those tasks lightened my step, as it was healing to
accomplish something with my hands, something I had
control over finishing. Up to that point, I had made it
through each day feeling as if I were in somewhat of a
holding pattern, not able to bring myself to start something new or finish anything completely. Now, with
clarity and success, I was able to inch forward again.

In a parallel timeframe, Mom was progressing
through her post surgery chemotherapy day by day, with
minimal energy. Her normal persona, that of a happy
woman bursting with energy, disappeared as her body
succumbed to poison from drugs that were killing off
the cancer cells while also having a noticeable impact on
her healthy cells. The drugs were impacting her ability to
eat, causing her tear ducts to clog, and nauseating her.

As she struggled day to day with these side effects,
Mom began to try to understand what she was supposed to be learning from this experience. In her journal, she wrote, "Cancer is about claiming my space,
having a right to be here on this earth, and appreciating
the contributions I make."

She kept track of her feelings each day, what she was able to manage, and whether she had any energy. One entry, the day after my birthday, she wrote, "What did I learn today? To be aware, notice things in my life, notice that I had a wonderful marriage, a warm feeling in my heart to know the power of love." Her choice to focus on the positive, even in the midst of her grueling situation, was a great example for me, one of many where she chose the glass-half-full path and carried on.

Mom continued to focus on healing and on May 13, she logged an update in her journal that said, "No more chemo!" It was a triumph for sure that she was finished poisoning her body and could now create space for her energy to come back little by little. The downside was that she stopped short of the recommended amounts of treatment. She never told me why she made that choice, but my sense was that she was just worn out from the drugs' effects and wanted to take her life back.

After I talked with Mom and heard this news, my happiness about her joy quickly transitioned to sadness as I recalled the clinical trial results I had read when she was first diagnosed. The clinical trials had found that there was only a 12 percent survival rate after five years for patients who were able to withstand all of the prescribed treatment, both pre- and post-surgery. These results were something I had filed away neatly in a box, but now—poof—there they were again, staring me in the face. I felt sick to my stomach as I started to feel even surer that the end would come—I just didn't know when. However, I chose not to share that information with my sisters or my mother. I wanted so much to honor Mom's joy in that moment.

Mom clearly wanted more than anything to move on, too; in the wake of her chemo, she always chose to focus on the positive strides she was making. On June 4, she logged an upbeat note in her journal: "First time more energy after watching TV in evening! Played bridge, had dinner, and cleaned up! Energy returning— thank you, God!"

Still, I couldn't shake the feeling that she needed more help than she realized, especially because her situation was taking a toll on my father, who was beginning to experience some health issues of his own. So, now that my home life and my new role at work were feeling more settled, I decided to fly back to Austin for a visit, to connect with Mom and understand better what was happening with Dad.

While I was there, Mom and I caught up on how she was feeling and on her ability to return to her normal activities, and our heart bond expanded even further. One day, we were able to get out of the house for a while to get pedicures and go shopping. As we were walking through the pharmacy section of Costco, she stopped and turned around suddenly. She had a big grin on her face as she said, "Rebecca, I have some exciting news to share. My radiation oncologist told me three days ago that the cancer was gone. I am cured!" She quickly turned away and continued looking for the vitamins she wanted to buy. It felt a little like a hide-and-seek game as she announced this news and transitioned back to her shopping right away.

Although I tried to maintain a happy facade, her comment shocked me, and I'm sure my surprise was painted on my face, which is probably why she moved right on and turned her head away. My first reaction was to question how her doctor was able to claim that she was cured of cancer so quickly. My understanding was that oncologists were not even permitted to use the word "cure"; they were supposed to say "remission."

Then I realized that Mom's choice of words was just that—her personal view of what the doctor had told her. I decided it was important in that moment to be supportive of the way Mom chose to express herself, even though inside I felt more like maybe she was healed only for now, at this point in time. I chose to focus on the moment and celebrate Mom where she was. She was relaxed and exuded joy. It warmed my heart.

We also went for a walk and enjoyed some time being totally comfortable in our own skin, authentic from the inside out. That day, I learned that my father's health was stable and he just needed his medication adjusted. At dinner that evening, Dad was able to laugh and tell jokes like a stand-up comic—something I had never experienced before. I wanted to bottle up the feeling of that day, cherish the joy and the comforting experiences, even if only for that moment in time.

Chapter 4:

A Passion for Learning

Always bear in mind that your own passion
to succeed is more important than any other.
—Abraham Lincoln

Over the summer of 2004, Mom continued to regain her strength and energy. She was able to start walking her three-mile path again around her neighborhood on Lake Austin, which fed her soul. She would even take a plastic grocery bag on her walks and pick up trash along her route. She was so focused on giving back, even in her exercise.

When I sat with the feeling that the experiences of the past year had jolted me enough to believe Mom might not be here much longer, I realized that if she were to pass on, I was not sure that I would know much about her life. I decided then that I wanted to know more, and I made a commitment to myself that I would ask Mom questions along those lines each time I went to visit her.

Some things I did know about Mom: She grew up as an only child in La Fountaine, Indiana, a town of six hundred people in Wabash County. Her father owned the only town garage and gas station. Her mother was on the city council. Mom was born in the Chinese year of the snake, which represents the intuitive, introspective, refined, and collected of the Chinese animal signs. Her favorite colors were purple and pink, and her lucky number was two, representing duality and duplication. Magnolias were her favorite tree, and peonies were her favorite flower. Mom was always ready to chart new and undiscovered territories and jump into any new activity with enthusiasm, and she was fascinated by endeavors that spoke to her intellect and filled her spirit with light.

On a trip to Austin in September 2004, I explored more about Mom's college years and other experiences that she believed had influenced her life most. I had just finished completing my master of business administration degree and was seeking new opportunities for growth myself, and because she had been such a strong role model for me growing up, I thought asking her questions would help me figure out more about my future path.

What I learned was amazing but not surprising. Mom was honored with Mortar Board membership in her senior year at Indiana University (IU). That same year, she was one of the founders of the Little 500 bicycle race, which still runs today. Mom was quite the overachiever, as she also founded her sorority while in college.

My dad was at IU, finishing his advanced degree, as Mom was completing her undergraduate degree. Mom and Dad met at an Indiana University event. Mom took another man as her date to this event, but Dad won her heart and they married eight months later. Dad's work took them to several new cities, starting with Cincinnati, Ohio, then Lubbock, Texas. Dad was working for Texas Tech University and was a dorm monitor. While in Lubbock, Mom helped found Mortar Board at Texas Tech University. I laughed out loud when she told me one generational story about living in Lubbock in the 1970s: she shared that Dad required her to dress up and wear a skirt to do the laundry. Mom thought this was quite extreme yet followed along to be compliant. I later learned that Dad wanted her to dress up to be a good example for the students. That was very much our dad, so I could see how he would have demanded something like that of Mom. I remember that same dad always wanting his daughters to be dressed up and presentable, just as he had requested of his new bride. We were to wear dresses and gloves whenever we went to dinner or to an event.

Mom's most influential teacher was Maxine, her piano teacher. Mom spent ten years learning piano from this gifted woman, starting at age nine. She spoke of Maxine as someone who provided a safe place to spend time, was very spiritual, and, mostly, allowed Mom to be herself. I imagine this kind of safe haven was a wonderful gift for Mom when she was growing up.

As I reflected on my years growing up in Houston, I never quite understood how Mom juggled her many demands of the day. She managed to raise five girls, all within eight years of age, while working full-time and cooking us breakfast and dinner every day. Dad traveled some for work, so she did all of that on her own some days during the week. I started to see some parallels between that and the new life I was creating, juggling the many demands of two small children, a big job, a home, and a dog. I realized that she had modeled the attitude for me that much could be accomplished in one day with focus and determination. I laughed internally at myself as I considered that I was becoming her in my new life, but it also felt comforting, as she was a tough act to follow.

Mom was an avid reader and loved learning. When I was in eighth grade, she enrolled in a master's program in child development, an on-the-job program in conjunction with where she worked at the Texas Medical Center. Children were her passion, and she yearned to learn more about the stages of their development. Mom incorporated the responsibilities of her advanced-level courses and homework, seemingly effortlessly, into her already full daily life.

Following the completion of her master's degree, she became the director of the childcare center of the Texas Medical Center. Though the center started out in a couple of temporary trailers, Mom dreamed of expanding it in order to serve more of the families in need who worked at the medical center. She diligently put together a plan and convinced the medical center leadership to buy some land and build a state-of-the-art child care center. Not surprisingly, Mom was able to build an effective case with a focus on meeting customer needs.

Mom led the opening of the newly designed center with a celebratory spirit and a palpable sense of accomplishment. Her eyes lit up when she talked about the project. The Texas Medical Center Child Care Center, in its new location, was the first childcare center in the United States to be open twenty-four hours a day, seven days a week, every day of the year. Word of the center's design and unique nature spread quickly. Mom traveled some to present examples of the research she had applied in the design and the results she had experienced, and the center quickly became a model for others to learn from.

In addition to her many skills, Mom was also a noteworthy seamstress. When I was in high school, she indulged my desire to design fancy dresses for formals. I had seven such dances my junior year. For each dance, I would draw the type of dress I wanted. We would then discuss options for fabric and go shopping. She would buy patterns sometimes, or alter ones she already had. It was a fun adventure for me and made me feel like a queen. She would make each dress for me happily and with ease. Mom was a great example of how to honor her loved ones' hopes and dreams.

After she had served in the childcare center leadership role for fifteen years, the direction of the medical center leadership started to change. Mom did not believe she would be able to maintain the high levels of quality and satisfaction she had been able to build. She decided it was time for a change, and she retired. Later, after moving to her home on Lake Austin, Mom explored new hobbies and talents and increased her focus on things she loved, like spending time on the water.

Her journal sums up things that made her heart sing: "canoe rides, boat rides, playing the piano, painting with watercolors, listening to music, reading, getting a massage, sharing with my women's group, talking to my loved ones, and simple abundance."

Mom was a loyal churchgoer, and while her faith was very strong, she also found a way to blend her spiritual beliefs with traditional Christianity. She was a passionate learner no matter the subject, always synthesizing seemingly unrelated topics to help expand her beliefs.

～☺～

In 2004, entering my second Christmas season as a divorced mom, I was feeling a little more healed and a little more comfortable in my new life. As I took stock of things, I was amazed and humbled by how much had changed and shifted over the past year. I had learned to adjust to my daily chaos, prioritizing the most important tasks, then sometimes reprioritizing in the moment. I still struggled with how to raise my two independent and stubborn children and continued to use the Love and Logic parenting philosophy to keep our conflicts at bay.

On December 18, snow was falling gently outside as I welcomed Mom and Dad for a visit in Boulder. Mom had enjoyed the past few months. She was feeling stronger, spending time doing what she loved, and putting herself first a little more. Dad was doing well also and in good health. He felt very authentic to interact with. He had been funny, nurturing, supportive, and loving recently to Mom and all of us. What a heartwarming Christmas gift to have them both in my home and to be able to enjoy some days with them alone before my children returned from their dad's house on Christmas Day.

The day after Mom and Dad arrived, I treated them to an anniversary dinner out at my favorite restaurant. We enjoyed reconnecting and laughing a lot, and the experience helped my heart expand a little more, pushing my edges and beliefs, as we celebrated the special relationship they had created over more than fifty wonderful years together.

The next day, Mom and I went for a tranquil walk in the snow. The snow glistened on the trees, and the crisp air kept our pace brisk. That afternoon, Dad joined us to go see the movie *Kinsey*, about a professor at Indiana University. It was my parents' idea to go. I had not been keeping up with movies very well and had no clue what I was stepping into. As the film began, I was shocked when I learned Kinsey was not just any professor but a sex researcher. It was quite an eye-opening experience to see such a provocative movie with my parents, now as an adult and a mother myself. It made me a little uncomfortable at first, but they found it fascinating to see a man they had both known while working at IU in Bloomington, around the time I was born. They both saw Kinsey's work as scientific, and that fed their analytical, intellectual side, but knowing the main character made the story more personal for them.

It was fun for me to learn through their perspective what life was like back then, a time when my father also worked at IU. My parents also knew Herman Wells, the IU president at the time, and when he appeared in the movie, they shared more stories and we all laughed. It was like I was peering into a little window into my parents' lives as young adults. It felt like another gift of knowledge and definitely expanded my views in an interesting way.

Later, we enjoyed a lovely dinner together and talked fairly openly about the movie, a first for me. The topic was a little awkward, yet Mom and Dad spoke of it from more of a scientific point of view. I slept better that night than I had in several months. Having both of them around, to share and teach me so much, warmed my heart.

∽◦Ꭷ◦∾

On Christmas morning, I awoke to a feeling of tightness in my chest and heart. I realized I was sad to not have my children back from their dad's yet. One of the things I loved most about Christmas was waking up and seeing the gleam in their eyes, the look of surprise and excitement. How supportive it felt to have Mom and Dad there, helping me through my first Christmas morning at home without my babies. Mom figured out quickly that I needed a distraction, so we set off to start cooking Christmas dinner.

Mom and I went for a walk after the presents were

wrapped and the baking was started. And then I noticed something about her that caught me off guard. She was using those little breathing exercises again, the ones she had used when her symptoms had first appeared, about eighteen months earlier. My heart sank. *No, it can't be. God, I am not ready for this.* Anger welled up inside my body. I had just finished enjoying several months of calm respite and now realized I had allowed a false sense of security to settle in—a belief that I was in control and Mom was healed.

Several times out of the corner of my eye, I watched Mom taking those short breaths, but when I asked if she was in pain, she quickly said no. Suddenly, my focus shifted, from my own sadness about missing my children to worrying about Mom. In that moment, I could feel that she was not okay, yet she was obviously not ready to talk about it. How scary it must have been for her to be in pain and not feel like she could tell me. How alone she must have felt.

When my children came home a few hours later, Mom wrapped them in her love, as she usually did, although this time, she seemed a little short with them. Mom had always focused so intently on my babies, making life all about them when she was around, indulging them in reading or painting or whatever they wanted to do. On this day, something was different.

I pulled her aside for a minute and wrapped my arm around her shoulder. I said, "Mom, I've been watching you, and you seem agitated, for some reason. It makes me sad to watch because I know this isn't how you normally interact. Is everything okay? I'm a little worried about you. I love you."

She looked at me for a moment as if she were going to tell me something big, but then she said only, "I'm fine, Rebecca, just tired from not sleeping well. I love you, too."

With the children back from their father's house, we opened presents and then enjoyed a lovely Christmas meal together as I tried to remain calm. As I processed the unfolding of the day, I realized our best next step was to enjoy the rest of Mom and Dad's visit, do things we had never tried, and create lasting memories. I quickly started to research activities in our area to figure out some options. Christmas lights were a favorite in our family, so we ventured out to see the light display at the Denver Botanical Gardens, a first for us since we'd lived in Colorado. Even though it was only forty degrees, we all enjoyed the walk through the gardens at night. The lighting display was more amazing than any I had ever seen. My children squealed with joy as they played hide-and-seek, and seeing the joy that illuminated Mom's face filled me with comfort and gratitude.

We awoke the next day to sun and warmer temperatures, so we all set out for a hike at Chautauqua Park. The trail was parallel to the striking Flatirons, a series of iron-ore hills sticking straight out of the side of the mountain in Boulder. We had looked at this distinctive feature of the Boulder skyline from the back deck of our home before, but the pace of our life had been so fast and furious since Leslie and I had moved to Boulder from California—starting with buying a house, adding on to it, having two children, and buying a second home, in the mountains—that exploring the actual hiking trails was another first for all of us.

Mom had also always wanted to go to the Pearl Street Mall, one of my favorite areas to window-shop and get ice cream with visitors, so we headed there next. The children played on the statues along the mall with Dad while Mom and I checked out a couple of stores. We discovered some amazing talent, many handmade items crafted from local artists. We bought some hand-painted Christmas ornaments that we both loved, matching in style yet each in our favorite color.

Then we went into an art gallery and a painting on the wall across the room grabbed my attention. My eyes zeroed right in on it. I had been looking for some artwork for my new home; I wanted something that was made locally and had a special meaning to me. As I stared at the wall, this piece seemed like the perfect option. The painting featured three panels of aspen trees positioned amid stones of several different, bright colors. The trees seemed to pop right out of the painting. Aspen trees are classically representative of Colorado, one of the few US states where aspens can thrive, largely because of its higher elevations and cooler temperatures, and the bright stones in the painting were so Boulder, very whimsical and fun.

Mom helped me negotiate a little on the price, and soon the painting was mine. The time to purchase some local artwork was right, as I was unsure whether this would be my last Christmas in Boulder. I was talking to the company where I worked about moving to a new position in a different state. As such, it would likely be the last time my parents would come to visit me in Colorado. In fact, it would be the last time for a lot of things, even though I didn't know that then.

Chapter 5:

Letting Go

If you don't like something, change it. If you can't change it, change your attitude.
—Maya Angelou

By the end of Mom and Dad's visit in Christmas 2004, Mom opened up about how she was feeling some pain again and knew something was wrong. She was going to see her doctor again when she returned to Austin. She was sad, knowing her perceived status as being cancer-free had changed, and she wasn't sure what was going to happen next. I chose to be strong for her, yet I struggled to keep my emotions in check. My memories of her clinical-trial results started to resurface. Here was another shift in her health status, this time representing something more widespread than her initial diagnosis.

Mom's doctor agreed that something was not right and ordered a PET scan. It was early January 2005. A few days later, Mom called to share the results from her scan. She said, "Rebecca, you know how I told you I was experiencing some pain and shortness of breath when we were together? The results I just got are not good. There's some activity showing up in my lungs. My doctor isn't sure what it is yet, but I'll keep you posted. I love you."

My heart sank. I was reminded again that her body was weaker this time and that this was the beginning of the end of her life as I knew it. I said, "Mom, thank you for calling and sharing the results. I know it's hard not to know what's going on. I'm here to support you. I love you."

I found it hard to focus on anything for more than a few minutes over the next couple of days. We were in a holding pattern as her doctor had ordered more tests, a CAT scan and some blood work, and we waited anxiously for the results. With my breathing short and my neck feeling tight, I braced for what I knew in my heart was not going to be good news.

Meanwhile, my discussions about a new role at my company had continued to progress. The position I was considering seemed to fit my skills well, and the leaders were very interested in my taking the job. However, because the job was in a different state, before it was possible for me to accept the new role, I first needed to negotiate with and secure agreement from my former husband to let me relocate with my children. As I processed these experiences unfolding one right after the other, I reflected for a moment on how I was handling the fast-paced, rapidly changing daily life that had become the norm for me, and I determined that having survived the events of the previous eighteen months, combined with the continued expansion of my heart, meant that maybe I was now strong enough to handle more. My recent experiences had proven to me that although life had taken different turns than I had imagined, my ability to believe that what was unfolding was positive gave me strength to continue my path and trust that changes I had perceived as obstacles were perhaps actually guiding me more toward authenticity.

Focusing on myself and my life for a moment, I allowed myself to dream a little about what was possible in my career and realized that something about this new job opportunity gave me energy and made my heart sing. I called my lawyer and inquired about the likelihood of securing court approval to move with my children. I felt a bit deflated as he informed me that the Colorado Supreme Court had ruled against a mother moving out of state in two other cases, similar situations, in which the mom was the primary provider for the children. My lawyer's recommendation was to convince my former husband directly, bypass the court system, and figure out something that mattered more to him to make this work.

Wow. He really thinks I'm capable of negotiating an agreement with a man who has taken the stance opposite mine on any topic related to our children since our divorce a year ago? Not so much, I thought. That type of agreement was legal and binding and seemed like quite an insurmountable task, definitely not in my direct control.

I paused and closed my eyes, cleared my mind, and asked for answers. I knew my best chance at an agreement was to engage my former husband in discussions with the help of our mediator assigned by the court to work with us on issues regarding our children, while I focused on the job opportunity that was unfolding on a parallel path. I knew it was time to turn this specific situation over to a higher power and rely more on my faith that this situation would work out in the best possible way for all of us. My stubbornness and strong will were learning to listen a little more and take a backseat, allowing my heart to lead and guide me forward. My part was to take the action I needed and become clear on what was important to me.

My priorities seemed very simple at this point in my life—what was becoming more important was to be present in each moment and passionate about what I was doing, how I was feeling, versus achieving some feat, holding a fancy title, or conquering the world. My heart-opening journey to authenticity felt solid.

～⊗～

My thoughts shifted back to Mom as we all awaited her test results. My earlier feeling that she was not long for this world began to kick around inside the box in which I had tucked it away so neatly. That box then shattered the day I answered the phone and heard Mom tell me, "Honey, the test results show nodules in my left lung. In order to figure out what the nodules are, I need to have a biopsy, which they've scheduled for next week."

Although Mom sounded calm and spoke quietly, I could hear the underlying fear in her voice as it cracked when she read the report to me. It didn't look like cancer on one report, but on another, it did, she said. I wondered what that really meant and how it was that they couldn't tell.

I sensed that Mom was in shock and didn't want to talk anymore, so I told her I loved her and hung up. I closed my eyes and visualized wrapping my arms around her, showering her with love, and prayed that God would fill her with grace. On one level, I had been preparing myself for the inevitable arrival of this day, and on another, I was in complete denial and full of surprise upon hearing these results. My heart ached for her, as I knew I had no control over the steps that would unfold next and that I had no power to change the outcome. I just needed to let go and honor Mom's journey as it unfolded.

Over the previous eighteen months, Mom had been very forthcoming with new information about her health status, every time she had new test results or saw her doctor. This time was different, as Mom had waited almost a week before sharing her PET scan results with me, in early January 2005. At the time, she told me that she had also spoken with my sisters, so I assumed they were also aware of what I knew. The test results showed that twenty tiny tumors were scattered throughout Mom's left lung, and that something abnormal was embedded in the lining.

As I thought about Mom, I could almost feel her fear of what might happen next. Her wondering whether this was the cancer spreading through her body and whether she would survive. I struggled to stay focused on my life at home through the weekend. I decided to shift my attention to my children and tried not to think of the news the next week would bring. I spoke with some of my sisters and kept the conversation light, even though I felt as if there were an elephant in the room with us. We stayed away from the topic of Mom and her health. Our family was prone to glossing over difficult subjects anyway and keeping a stiff upper lip when situations were tough; plus, I thought my sisters knew about the outcome of Mom's test results and just didn't want to talk about it. However, after hanging up with each of them, I started to wonder if that was true. Over the past year, some of us had started to rely on one another and share more of our pain openly, so I wasn't sure whether they were reverting to old norms or really did not know the details of Mom's test results.

On Monday, I went to work and was let down by the news that the job I was being considered for had been offered to someone else. I had allowed myself to feel the life-giving energy that this job process was feeding me, the chance to use my mind in a strategic way. All signals pointed to the idea that the role was meant for me. Every time I had interviewed and asked for feedback, all reports had been glowing.

As I processed this disappointing news, I felt as if my heart were breaking in two. Here it was, a promise of something new, a fresh start, and all of a sudden, the door was slammed shut. Or so I felt inside. Mom had taught me growing up that when doors were closed or my dreams were not realized, it was God's way of protecting me from things that were not right or would have been harmful. As much as I felt in my heart that something was not right for me in this job, tears of disappointment flowed down my face. However, as sad as I was, I knew I needed to turn the process over to a higher power and refocus my attention on Mom.

❦

I awoke Tuesday and imagined holding my mom in my love as she headed in for her biopsy. A few hours later, one of my sisters called, very upset. She had just found out about Mom's test results, which, evidently, Mom had shared only with me at first. I sat there feeling surprised and not sure what to do next, conflicted and a little self-absorbed. I felt special on some level that Mom had confided only in me, yet at the same time I felt awkward that no one else knew.

When I checked in with Mom later that afternoon, she was worn out and her voice was weak. She shared that the procedure had taken all day, as the doctor had also tried to implant a PICC line while conducting the biopsy, to make it easier for her to manage the chemo-therapy that would likely come next. But the fact that her body was dehydrated had made it impossible for the implant process to work. She was frustrated and angry that she had wasted a day inside. As I tried to comfort her and calm her down, she shared that she would receive the results of the biopsy a few days later, on Friday of that week. Knowing how scared she was about what the results might show, I offered to be at her side when she went to her doctor for the biopsy results. I could hear the relief in her voice when she responded that she would take me up on my suggestion. I flew in two days later, on Thursday afternoon, around four o'clock.

When I arrived in Austin, Mom allowed me into her inner world, keeping me very close over the follow-ing two days. She picked me up from the airport alone, which was a first; it was a tradition in our family for both Mom and Dad to come get any of us from the airport. I was delighted with the special gift of seeing her first one-on-one and warming up our conversation on the way back to her house. That night, I helped her cook dinner, which, I realized upon reflection, I had never really done with her before. I had always enjoyed baking desserts, so my sisters had been the ones to help Mom with dinner. But that night, she wanted it to be different, and she asked me to assist her, so I did. It felt as if we were in our own little pocket of space, spend-ing time together while the world stood still.

The next morning as we were walking out the door to go to the doctor's office, I was quite surprised to learn that Mom had told my father he did not need to come. She really wanted him to go play bridge and enjoy his morning. I felt quite awkward as I followed her out to the car and my dad stood in the doorway. How scared Mom must have been if she had not wanted to trouble my father. There she was, still taking care of others, as her health status continued to deteriorate.

Mom and I drove to the appointment mostly in silence. I focused on remaining calm and strong for her. The stillness was almost deafening. A nurse led us into the examination room, where my sister Susan joined us. As Mom's doctor entered the room, I could see the concern in his eyes. Mom sat on the table and I stood right at her side, with my arm around her shoulder. I was facing her doctor as he lit up the X-ray on the box to the left of her and displayed it for us. As he began to speak, he looked at the scan. It must have been one of those very difficult moments for a specialist in his field of work. He said those twenty-plus little tumors were definitely cancer and it was spreading through her lungs. If only this were her breast cancer, he said, he could treat her with hormones, but he had looked into that with her doctor in Houston, and it wasn't possible. This was her rectal cancer, now metastasized. And radiation was not an option, because of the multiple tumors. Chemotherapy was the only course of treatment, and he had only one or two drugs to offer—the same drugs that had made her sick the year before, sick enough that she'd had to go to the emergency room one day with dangerously low potassium levels.

My sister put her arm around Mom's left side, and we held her close as we processed the results. We paused for what seemed like an eternity in that silent space. Then the doctor spoke again. He said he needed to run one more test: a bone scan. As much as I wanted to burst into tears, I knew I needed to be strong and focus on supporting Mom at that time. I took some deep breaths and kept my arm around her shoulder as we walked out to the car.

In late January 2005, the week after her biopsy, Mom bravely endured her bone scan. The results were good and tough at the same time. The good news was that the cancer was not present anywhere on the bone-scan results. The tough part was that she needed to be on chemotherapy drugs for the rest of her life in order to stay alive.

Mom considered her reality and decided she would try chemotherapy again. If it made her sick, she would stop. She wanted to expand her treatment options and chose to embrace alternative medicine in addition to the chemotherapy. She researched options and chose weekly acupuncture treatments and Chinese herbs. On some level, she probably knew that the drugs would have the same effect as before and wanted to be prepared. She chose to add some Eastern-medicine treatments to her routine in order to enhance her comfort and hopefully prolong her life.

Most people would have taken the news over the previous couple of weeks of early 2005 very hard and would have fallen into a deep depression. Mom could have wallowed in self-pity about why this was happening to her and become completely consumed with her pain and sadness. Instead, she chose to accept her situation and prognosis and carry on with her normal life in as feasible a way as she could, given her health status.

As one of Mom's passions was giving back, including being involved in her local neighborhood association, the weekend following her bone scan, while her cancer was metastasizing through her body, she spent a day outside, building a new open-space trail with one other person in her neighborhood. She was happiest in nature and felt accomplished when the trail was complete, maybe because it was something she was able to control. In all she did, despite any circumstances, Mom showed a strength and determination that seemed to overpower any illness, even metastasized cancer.

As Mom started on the chemotherapy drugs, she became very sick again, just as before. She was unable to keep down any solid food. Her eyes dried out, and she developed sores in her mouth. Propel was the only drink she was able to stomach. I wanted her to come visit Boulder in February 2005, but the chemotherapy was making her hands and feet cold, so I knew it was probably not a great idea. However, I wanted to see her again soon, so I decided I would plan my next trip to Austin to be over a Thursday night so I could go with her and hear live music at a new place she had discovered. In addition to spending more time in nature, Mom was filling her heart with music more and in different ways. She was practicing letting go of her health condition and experimenting with new experiences that gave her joy.

As Mom was considering stopping the IV portion of her chemotherapy regimen, her doctor offered up an experimental drug as an option, so she researched the outcomes. Even if this drug were effective, it would prolong her life for only about four months. No thank you, she said. She decided to take her chances on her own, without the help of any Western medicine. Her goal was to live a high quality of life for whatever time she had left. She was very comfortable with her decision, yet it left the rest of us in a space of deep concern and sadness about how the next steps would unfold.

Mom continued her alternative therapies, and her energy increased. Pretty soon, she starting taking walks again. She researched special diets that had been proven to reduce cancer's ability to thrive and grow. As she considered how to change her diet, she realized she would have to stop eating certain foods. Foods heavy in saturated fats, such as filet steak and bacon, were such favorites of hers that she was not willing to stop eating them. Mom wanted to live her life the way she wanted, even if it meant her time on Earth would be shorter. She was so very strong, every step of the way, even as my concern about what would happen next deepened.

With her chemotherapy complete only a couple of months after her biopsy results, Mom continued to explore her passion for learning, always seeking to understand, and increased the number and variety of books she was reading. Mom wanted to understand what the disease in her body represented. Even though she had survived late-stage breast cancer some twenty years before, she was now facing a more formidable opponent, a cancer that had a lot more strength than she had experienced the first time. She applied her passion for learning to discovering more about the mind-body connection. Was it her thoughts that were keeping the cancer alive? She read Louise Hay's book *Heal Your Body* and thought there might be some truth to that idea.

As Mom continued her research over the course of another year, she documented what she learned and her thoughts about it in her journal. She started to believe that any discomfort in her body was a direct message to her about where she was out of alignment with her true self. In one of her passages, she recorded the following: "Guidance came in the form of discomfort, if she would only be still and listen." Mom uncovered that maybe the quiet, negative voices in her "noisy mind"—negative self-talk about what she needed to do and should have done—were part of the reason for her discomfort, keeping her always second-guessing internally.

On her journey to heal her body and conquer the cancer, she continued to learn about and try different types of healing. Kimberly, her acupuncturist, told Mom about a Buddhist monk who was to visit Austin in several months. He was known to have healing powers, and Kimberly had a connection that would enable Mom to see him.

Mom was so excited about visiting with the monk. I accompanied her to the temple and went inside to wait in a calm and inviting front room. The walls were painted mint green, and the chairs and sofa were beige, made of soft velvet. A fountain in the corner of the room provided relaxing sounds as the water trickled down the wall. Mom went back for her visit with the monk alone not long after we arrived. Afterward, as we drove back home, she told me about the experience.

She described it as having evoked a feeling similar to being in the presence of the purest light that existed.

Throughout her quest to understand more, Mom brought in new ideas and considered them while balancing them with her strong faith and Christian upbringing. To her, faith was the great lever of life. Without it, humans could do nothing; with it, all things were possible.

While I processed the events of the first month and a half of 2005 and all that had changed during that time, I sought to maintain a calm state and started to feel myself detaching from my emotions and the reality that was unfolding. I was still trying to understand why this time was different, how it was that Mom was suffering quietly inside—it seemed so unfair that this was happening to someone who gave so much, who loved so deeply from her heart—but as the reality of Mom's condition and the loss of the job I had thought was perfect for me sank in, I continued my practice of letting go and trusting my path. I believed that my heart-opening journey to authenticity would continue if I focused in my heart on believing the best next step for me would emerge at the right time.

Still, I felt conflicted between pursuing those goals and giving in to my fear about Mom dying. I sat quietly with these feelings and meditated with my go-to verse: "be still and know that I am God." Repeating this mantra over and over calmed me enough to fall asleep at night.

In late February, I received a call from my friend Frank, my company's sales leader in Nashville. He had a new job opportunity for me to consider. I had met Frank in my previous consulting role, when I had worked with some of his clients. He said he had felt the void of my consulting skills with his clients and had figured out a way to carve out a strategic role for me in a new, long-term contract he had just signed with his largest healthcare client. The downside was that the job was in Nashville and was only for one year.

I chose to let go of those seemingly insurmount able details and pray for a path forward. This role held much more promise than the last one he had brought to me and was an even better fit for my skills. I also welcomed the distraction from my sadness about Mom's illness. I shifted my focus to the possibility of using my strategic mind again and ventured into another interview process.

Chapter 6:

A New Chapter Unfolding

*Just when you think you know exactly
how it's going, some unexpected possibility
shows up and it begins to get even better.*
—Andre Pough Sr.

In early March 2005, I flew to Austin to celebrate
Mom's birthday. We all went out to hear live music
and spend quality time together. I shared with her my
excitement about the potential new work role that had

surfaced for me. Although I knew the fact that the job was located in another state and was only a one-year commitment could prove to be prohibitive, the position was intriguing enough for me to continue to consider it.

As I thought about the possibility of using my strategic mind again, I ventured to push past any constraints my mind brought forward. I started to wonder if the role could be expanded into something more comprehensive, something that was worthy of a move to a new state. I realized in that moment, as I was sharing the story with Mom, that experiencing the disappointment of losing the previous job opportunity had actually furthered my practice of letting go of outcomes and allowing the process of my life experiences to unfold with a higher power at the helm.

Mom was delighted about the prospect of a new chapter unfolding for me. She said, "Oh, Rebecca, you have been so deserving of a job that you are passionate about for over a year now. After all you have been through with Leslie and sacrificing for your children, it feels like the right time for you to make this change. I am so excited for you!"

I responded, "Thank you, Mom. Something I am always able to count on is your positive encouragement and support. That means so much to me. The kids and I are going to go visit Nashville over spring break. Would you and Dad be able to join us? It would be extra special to explore this new city together."

Mom replied that she thought that would be fun, and we started making plans for the trip to Nashville together. My children and I met Mom and Dad there in mid-March and had a wonderful and yet emotional time together. I was grateful to have the gift of my parents helping my children and me explore the city, grateful that Mom felt strong enough to travel and healthy enough to be playful with my children.

Our first full day there, we walked a few blocks from our hotel to Centennial Park. The sun was shining, and the temperatures were in the mid-seventies. We started out on a walking trail that circled the park. We passed a large pond with a fountain in the middle and orange tiger lilies blooming at the edges. We stopped there as the kids ran up to throw stones into the water with Mom. As I sat there watching them, I remembered a special time from my own childhood. When I was about four years old, my mom's dad came to live with us in Houston. He loved to fish. We often went to Herman Park so we could feed the ducks and he could teach us how to fish.

My daughter snapped me back to the present by tugging on my pant leg, asking if I had any bread to feed the ducks. I felt an immediate warmth for this new place, as that memory comforted my soul.

Mom was strong until the third night of the trip but then became very sick to her stomach. She started throwing up and was unable to leave the bathroom. It was a rude awakening to experience her being so sick all of a sudden. Over the previous three days, we had enjoyed moments of being at the highest highs, like a hot-air balloon floating across the sky. Pure joy and love had radiated through our bodies as we celebrated this new place we were discovering and the excitement of Mom's being able to be there with us. But that night, Mom's body reminded all of us of the cancer spreading through it. My heart grew heavy and that hot-air balloon deflated as I struggled with how to help her, how to be supportive. My detached state quickly transitioned to reconnecting with my deep pain about what was to come next, the big unknown we all knew and yet feared. And because my heart had had more practice at being open in my day-to-day experiences, I experienced these feelings even more acutely. As I sat on the bed in my hotel room, waiting for Mom to come out of the bathroom, I knew I just needed to be patient and hope that she would regain her strength.

We were all grateful that Mom awoke the next day strong enough to explore some more. We visited a church and enjoyed lunch at a locally owned restaurant, and then flew home to our separate cities. On the plane, I concentrated on my potential move and started to make a list of all the tasks I would have to complete in order to move my children and me to another state. The doing part of preparing for the move kept my mind from focusing on the reality of what was happening with Mom and was a welcome distraction for the moment.

It also helped that my new job held such promise and the possibility of expansive joy for me. For the first time in my life, I was fully engaged in the transition, asking questions of my future manager and seeking to understand more details of this new role, my responsibilities, and what success would look like, while trusting that the best outcome was unfolding for all. And while I was busy going through the motions, the universe moved some very large mountains to clear the path for my new chapter to begin—mountains that my friends and even my lawyer said could not be moved.

Once I let go and turned over the handling of these seemingly immovable mountains to a higher power, the answer came to me one day. I figured out the key to negotiations with my former husband and convinced him to let me move with the children to Nashville, while still giving him what he wanted out of the arrangement. My tightened shoulders started to relax as I felt the power of this accomplishment. Yes, I *was* capable of the impossible if I allowed others to help and influence me.

Once the big obstacles about moving were out of the way, I negotiated a broader role, the one I had envisioned earlier as I dreamed of the possibilities. I convinced a couple of executives at my company to create a new position for me, pay for my move to Nashville, and allow me start a new advisory-services consulting practice that I would lead. As I presented the business case, the positive feedback flowed with ease and my path forward was seemingly orchestrated by design.

I paused for a moment and felt the deep joy and comfort in my heart. I knew I had had help—though much of it was unexplainable in words and could only be felt—with all of these details falling into place. It was an expansion of my faith, a journey beyond the edges of all I knew—at least, that is how I came to explain the clearing that unfolded over a month's time, the wonder and miracles wrapped up together and all for me—a good reminder of what Mom taught me about doors closing. Through the process, I was focused on the moment day-to-day and moving on to the next step, working through each piece of the puzzle from a place of unfiltered faith. Those puzzle pieces all fell into place over a month's period as I managed all of my interactions from the purest self I had ever shown to the outer world.

A few weeks later, I started my new position and traveled back and forth as I looked for a new home. I was blessed with some valuable advice from a coworker Don, a Nashville native, on where to look for homes and how to navigate the city. After many tours in several neighborhoods, I finally landed on the house I wanted, one that did not fit the "criteria" that my real estate agent had identified for me. I had thought I needed the same-size house I had owned in Boulder, one with four bedrooms, four baths, and a garage. Every time I had researched homes for sale on my computer, this house was at the top of the list. We drove by it several times on our journey to look at other houses. I finally asked Velvet, my real estate agent, to show me the house. She had said the reason we had not looked at it was that it was a three-bedroom, two-bath house with no garage. Despite its smaller size, I felt something drawing me to this house. The moment I stepped onto its original mahogany hardwood floors, my heart was filled with peace and I felt like I was home. The house was built in 1950 and, in addition to the floors, featured many charming older design details, such as a separate door to the kitchen for deliveries.

I closed on the house in early May 2005. Mom was feeling strong again, and she really wanted to help me move in. I knew she was not strong enough to help with boxes, but that was not important to me at the time. Being able to share the beginning of my new life chapter in this lovely new city with my sweet mother and enjoying each experience without any other distractions was the treasure I was after.

We decided on Mother's Day weekend as a good time for her to come visit. My children were still in school back in Boulder. Their father had graciously agreed to take care of them as I spent time starting my new job and closing on my new home.

I felt in my heart that this might be one of those moments in life that would never be repeated. I really had no sense of what the experiences would bring, although I felt sure they would be etched in my memory forever. And how deeply moved and touched I was by what unfolded that weekend.

Before Mom came, we talked on the phone to firm up our plans. After we finalized the logistics, she surprised me by saying, "Rebecca, I would like to know what you would want of mine to keep after I am gone. I have picked out things with your sisters, although you have not asked for anything."

I was both touched by her thoughtfulness and a little scared by her request, more because of my lingering fear about what it would be like when she passed from her physical state. I responded, "Mom, that is such a thoughtful thing for you to ask. What I really want from you is what you want me to have. Something special to you. Something you pick out just for me."

She was a little surprised that I did not have a list picked out. Amid all the loss and letting go I had already endured in dividing many things between two homes in my divorce, I had become more comfortable with not having much attachment to material things. I was most interested in something shared from her heart, something that would have special significance for me every day forward.

She said, "Thank you for letting me know. I will pick out some special things to bring. I'm so excited about seeing your new house and spending Mother's Day with you, just the two of us. I'll talk to you soon. I love you."

When Mom arrived in Nashville, she beamed as she talked about the adventure we were about to enjoy. We stayed at a hotel down the street on Friday night. The next morning, we went to my new home to meet the moving van. I walked her through the house quickly to show her where I wanted to put things, where my bedroom was, and where the kids wanted their beds to be. The house had two bedrooms and a bath upstairs. I had thought that would work well, as the kids wanted to have their own rooms, but when we had discussed the new home, the kids had corrected me and said they wanted to share a bedroom. Here was another positive sign that this was the right place for us.

I marked off items out front, signed off on the moving papers, and went inside. The movers had set up the beds for us, and we were able to find the box with the sheets fairly quickly. Up in the guest room where she was staying, Mom and I started to unpack the necessities for that evening. After we made her bed, she asked me to sit on it with her for a moment.

She walked over to her suitcase and pulled out a bag. She said, "Rebecca, I picked out some things to give you. It took me a while to go through my jewelry, as I wanted to pick just the right pieces for you." As I sat on the bed and watched her, she unwrapped several items one by one and shared the story about each.

As she unwrapped one gold pin, memories from my childhood came flooding back to me. The pin was the shape of a bird with tiny rubies at the base of the bird's legs. "Mom, I remember that pin from when I was at Harmon School and you worked there when I was little. You used to love it! You wore it so much. Wow—it's so special that you want me to have it. Thank you!" As she continued to unwrap the remaining pieces, I felt honored—they were way more meaningful than anything I could have thought of myself or chosen on my own. Each item felt like a gift designed to touch my heart in a way that I could not even express in words.

The next morning, Mother's Day, we woke up early, drank our coffee, and discussed the best way to prioritize the major unpacking project I was facing. Mom said unpacking the kitchen first would help me to feel settled. She also wanted to make sure I was prepared for the children's move a couple of weeks later, after school let out in Boulder.

Setting up a kitchen was not anything I had ever paid much attention to. Growing up, my sisters had spent more time cooking with Mom than I, and while I had been married, my former husband had been the main chef in our home and had been the one in charge of the kitchen. I felt unprepared and inadequate as I grappled with how to organize everything in my new space. Mom thoughtfully explained how to set up a kitchen in a way that flowed with how you used it. This included keeping some things low for the children. She was always thinking of others, even when she was sick. As we unpacked, she and I talked about what it felt like for her to wake up each day not knowing if it would be her last. "Mom, I would like to know more about what you are going through each day, would you describe more how it feels?" She smiled and obliged, although it was still hard for her to talk about herself. "Rebecca, some days I feel strong in the morning and out of breath in the afternoon. Those days I take time to appreciate the leaves swaying on the trees as I look out over the lake from our back porch." She stopped for a minute as the weight of this conversation was settling in. "Other days it is harder for me to get out of bed early like I am used to doing. As I lay in bed, I think of the many joys that have filled my life, mostly your father and you girls. What helps me get through those tough days is saying my favorite Bible verse, Psalm 23. It gives me comfort." I walked over and wrapped my arms around her as tears poured down both of our cheeks, feeling the depth of emotion of new beginnings mixed with unknown timing of endings.

After a few hours of unpacking, we were ready for a break. It was a sunny, warm day, so we decided to go have a picnic. We stopped at a store to pick up some sandwiches and drinks, and somehow she snuck away from me to buy something, without my noticing. When we got home, she startled me by handing me a box. I opened the box and found a coffee mug with the inscription "the soul would have no rainbow if the eyes had no tears." The sentiment touched me deeply; it was so loving, and straight from Mom's heart. The words on the mug reminded me of one of the most valuable perspectives Mom had raised me to believe: that I should embrace the challenges in my life as opportunities for personal growth and always trust that difficult times yielded new beginnings and blessings. Little did I know how true those words would ring over the next year.

∽◉∽

Two weeks went by quickly, and I began to settle into my new home a little each day. It was June 2005; school was out by then and my children were in our home, at my side. I chose to spend one weekend connecting the stereo so we could enjoy music and started unpacking the children's toys. They were much happier, more relaxed and secure, once they could see their toys and other belongings in their new space. It made a huge difference to them to be able to touch some of the things they had said goodbye to as we had packed up in Boulder.

On Saturday afternoon that weekend, I caught up with one of my sisters and heard some unsettling news—something I knew in my heart yet had been keeping tucked away as I managed my move and the start of my new job. Mom's local oncologist in Austin had shared with my sister that her cancer was fast growing and there was nothing any of us would be able to do to change her condition. He recommended loving her and spending as much time with her as we were able, and appreciating her life and all that had been.

Those were very heavy-feeling words as I received them and started to process what they really meant in my heart. I said to my sister, "Thank you for giving me this update. I really appreciate your being so open with me and sharing these details. It helps me feel close, even though I am not able to be there." While it was not what I wanted to hear, it was definitely something I knew it was time to face.

A few more weeks of unpacking and getting acclimated to our new lives went by, and I felt a little lighter having cleared out even more boxes. As I made my way through another box, I came across an article on grief, which my therapist in Boulder had given to me. It looked like just another piece of paper at first, yet once I began reading it, I felt frozen in time. A well of grief formed in my throat and heart as I started to read the article. Sentence by sentence, the reality that this time was it and that my mom was really dying hit me hard. I sat still and closed my eyes as tears poured down my checks. I felt as if I were in two parallel universes, struggling with the internal conflict of experiencing the heaviness of my mom's deteriorating health in one universe and the upbeat joys of the new life I was creating in Nashville in the other. I knew I needed to feel supported by someone, someone who would understand this feeling, so I called my sister Karen and read the article to her. We both cried as we discussed the impending change and deep loss that was about to unfold.

Crying and talking with my sister helped me realize that I had sunk into somewhat of a depressed state as I had put these feelings on hold for months. Now that I was in my new space and my physical transition was complete, I was able to be still and let the sadness flow, to allow my feelings and my fear of the unknown to have a voice. And I realized that I probably needed to reach out for help locally and start learning how to handle what was happening.

I went to the computer and started researching local resources for coping with losing a loved one to cancer. I discovered several options and ventured into an unknown space for me: a cancer support group. Because I grew up in a family of five children, most of my early life took place in some kind of group, so I felt comfortable in numbers starting when I was young. Yet I had never been part of a support group with people I didn't know. Still, I was feeling so raw with pain that I was willing to try something new.

As I considered my options, I chose Gilda's Club, a group with a mission to ensure that all people impacted by cancer are empowered by knowledge, strengthened by action, and sustained by community. I looked up the meeting schedule and planned to attend a meeting when I could find a babysitter. I was nervous as I drove myself to the meeting, even though I was becoming more comfortable trying new things and had been pleasantly surprised by the outcomes of those efforts.

I walked into the room, met the leader, and sat down. When I started to introduce myself to the group, I spoke barely five words before tears started flowing down my cheeks. *Yes, I am definitely in pain if I feel comfortable enough to show my emotions to total strangers*, I thought. The good news was that I was not alone—I was surrounded by others who were also feeling sadness and pain.

I listened to the other five people in the group share their stories of how cancer had impacted their lives and where they were on their own journeys. Then it was my turn. I spoke of the reality that my mom was dying yet no one was able to tell me when it would happen. I shared stories about the events of the past six months and how I felt out of control. I then was able to talk about how special it was for me to be at her side when she learned that her cancer had metastasized and how lucky I felt to have been able to share special experiences with Mom every month since that moment of truth in January 2005.

As I shared these stories with the group, the heaviness in my gut, my fear of the unknown, started to dissipate. I had reached outside my inner circle of family and friends for help, and my learning to cope had begun.

That night, as I drove home from Gilda's Club, I felt full of gratitude and warmth. I realized that I was appreciating Mom for who she was in the moment, and appreciating my ability to be fully present for her. I was honoring her journey and accepting her path. I decided I wanted to ask Mom more details about what life was like for her each day. As I processed and felt the support-group experience in my mind, I was relieved for the opportunity to sit with people like me, to learn that I was not alone in facing tough situations and trying to get through them.

As I sat with the support-group experience, I realized I had shared details about my situation with the other participants, yet I had not talked about my feelings of sadness and impending loss. Instead, I had spoken from my mind, in an intellectual way, using an approach that was still more comfortable for me and kept me detached from my current reality. Then, as I tried to actively transition from my thinking self to my feeling self, I asked myself if I really felt comfortable in a group setting. The answer was clear and bold. *No, not really.* The truth was, I was facing the greatest loss one can experience, a deep loss of the heart, yet in the group setting, I had reverted to describing my situation from a mental state. It felt too complicated to describe to these total strangers my story of Mom's cancer and how it was impacting my life. All I wanted was to fall apart, let my emotions flow, and have someone I cared about hold me. The person I had become was more interested in feeling supported from my heart, versus having someone fix me or make the pain go away. I was also feeling selfish, as I did not care about listening to someone else's story. What I really learned through the support group was that at that point in my life, I needed my support to be all about me.

I went to sleep reflecting on my experience and decided I would start looking for a grief counselor to guide me through this journey. In the early hours of the next morning, I awoke suddenly from a dream. I sat straight up in bed, feeling a little out of sorts yet clear in my mind about what I had seen in my dream. I had watched Mom die in her sleep, sometime before dawn, in a very peaceful way. By now, I had learned to trust my intuition and the messages that came to me in my dreams. While this experience a few years before would have been very frightening for me, the dream gave me comfort in the form of knowledge about how Mom would die. But I still had no answers about when.

Chapter 7:

Treasuring Each Moment

*Happiness is not found in things you
possess, but in what you have the courage
to release.*
—Nathaniel Hawthorne

My children and I went to Austin for the week of
the Fourth of July, one of Mom's favorite hol-
idays. We enjoyed spending time on the lake with full
abandon, allowing the days to unfold spontaneously
and following Mom's lead. Not knowing when the
time would come for Mom to leave us, we wanted to

enjoy this time to the fullest, as if it would be our last Fourth of July celebration with her.

Mom always loved seeing the children's eyes light up with various fireworks we set off from their boat dock on Lake Austin. She always bought sparklers, "dancing" chicks, and rainbow fountain fireworks, and every year we tried out some new kinds as well. Mom and the kids worked together to bake her special chocolate cake. She was very patient with my children as they decorated it together, giving both my son and my daughter ample opportunities to taste-test some of the homemade icing.

I was also able to spend some quality one-on-one time with Mom. Most days, I accompanied her on her usual three-mile walk around her neighborhood. The route took her up some steep hills, and I was amazed to see her still tackling them. Her pace was slower, and she added some stops along the way, but it was nonetheless an incredible feat for someone in her condition.

As we walked the first day, we climbed the first hill and stopped to take in the view overlooking Lake Austin. She was a little out of breath, so I waited a few minutes. Then I asked, "Mom, have you ever thought about what your greatest life accomplishments are? To me, they are countless and full of impact. I'm just curious if you've ever thought about them yourself."

She smiled at me, looking a little puzzled, and said, "Well, raising the five of you girls, without anything major happening to any of you or without much help or support, is probably what I would say."

We walked a little farther, and at our next resting point, I looked at her and smiled. "Mom, who have been the people in your life who have influenced you most?"

I was surprised by her response. She said, "Well, I would probably say my mother and father had the biggest impact on me, for encouraging me to go to college. That was in the late 1940s, and many women were encouraged to focus on getting married and having children, versus going to college. I felt it was a special gift to have my mom and dad support my interest in education."

Mom then shared that she considered college a turning point in her life, for many reasons. She had been away from home for the first time, able to try new things on her own and gain confidence in herself. She had had the opportunity to become involved in many new types of activities and forge new friendships. She felt most like college had expanded her views and given her a place to enrich her knowledge.

We walked more and came around to the top of the last hill, and I began to focus my questions on the present. I wrapped my arm around her shoulder and said, "Mom, I know you've had a lot of time to think lately. I'm wondering if you've thought at all about how you would want to be remembered when it is time for you to leave us."

With that, the mood shifted a bit and I could tell I had caught her off guard. She talked a little about wanting to be cremated and having her ashes spread over the lake, yet she spoke of it somewhat in the past tense. The topic of conversation was deep and introspective, and I decided it was time to take a break.

In order to bring some levity to the discussion, I transitioned to a different type of conversation, one in which I was able to give her some feedback and share some things about her that awed me. I said, "Mom, I just want you to know how amazing you are to me. I have never seen anyone get as much done in a day as you can. And you do it with a smile on your face."

She listened very intently as I described how it felt to be supported by her. She wanted to know more and in what way. I continued in detail, talking about her as a woman, a mother, a grandmother, a working mom, a wife, a Stephen Ministry representative, and a self-healer. Mom sometimes struggled with receiving praise or being called out in a setting of more than one person for her incredible gifts, but this time she soaked up every word as it left my mouth. I told her I would write down all of these thoughts so she could read about all of her gifts again, and she smiled.

Later, I found a journal entry from around this time in her journal that sums up her desire to be worthy and to accept the best: "I am willing to release the need to be unworthy. I am worthy of the very best in life, and I now lovingly allow myself to accept it." While outwardly we could see that she always wanted to be in the background, just quietly and selflessly giving to others, I didn't realize until then what deep feelings of unworthiness she harbored inside. She masked that well.

〰◯〰

Throughout the fall of 2005, Mom and I continued our talks about her childhood and other things she remembered. She said, "Everyone in our town knew Mom and Dad. Dad was always helpful in fixing people's cars at the garage and gas station he owned. Mom was looked up to as one of the leaders on the city council. When we walked down Main Street from our house, everyone would always say hello and smile, as if we were royalty or something."

Mom's energy became a little stiff as she continued. Growing up as an only child in a small town, she perceived that her mother went to extremes to ensure that her only daughter did not grow up spoiled. As Mom gave me examples of the way her mother had raised her, I could sense her pain, so I changed the subject and asked about her grandparents. "Mom, tell me more about Arthur and Dora Annetta. All I know is that Dora Annetta died the morning I was born."

As she spoke of Annetta, Mom's eyes lit up and she shared, "I really enjoyed learning how to smock and make quilts with her. She was also the first person who introduced me to the concept of healing through natural means, such as catching rainwater and making a healing drink to cure an upset stomach." She then stopped for a moment and looked at me. I was not sure what she was going to say next. Mom described for me how I reminded her of Annetta and how she wished I could have known her. Mom had given me Annetta's china a few years earlier. It had felt like a special gift at the time, and now, in this moment, knowing that I had it made me even more grateful.

Learning more helped me feel more connected to Mom and helped keep my fear at bay, at least for a while. The experience also helped me give to Mom in ways she could receive and filled my heart with joy in the process. By choosing to be so vulnerable, to open her life to me in a comfortable and selfless way, Mom continued to facilitate my heart-opening journey with her openness and candor.

During the last months of 2005, the doctor reported that her cancer markers were increasing and that there was nothing any of us could do about it. Mom didn't seem very interested in the reports. She mainly wanted to enjoy each day to its fullest. She was such a great role model for me, even in this situation. She was always teaching, always seeking to enjoy life, not knowing what would come tomorrow, packing every possible experience that would fit into a day, and treasuring each moment.

As 2006 arrived, I took stock of all that had gone on over the past two years. I had survived a divorce with two young children, had come close to losing my job a couple of times, had successfully navigated the details of moving to a new state with my children as a divorced mom without primary custody, and now faced my sweet mother's being sick again with cancer. But here she was, still around, two years later. Quite the fighter, she was determined to live her life as she wanted to. And she was still with us despite the reality of her condition, largely because of her resolve in guiding her own path toward healing, versus a path designed by traditional Western medicine. I was amazed that she was still with us, although also aware that this could not continue forever.

Sure enough, a couple of weeks into 2006, I was reminded that things were changing. January 11 was a stormy night in Nashville, full of lightning and strong winds and rain. As I walked to my bedroom, I passed the familiar pictures on the wall of my mom as a child, my father and his brother as young boys, my parents' wedding picture, and a picture of my maternal grandfather's garage. It was something I did several times a day without noticing the photographs, but now, all of a sudden, something was different. As I walked down this same hallway, Mom's baby picture fell off the wall onto the rug in front of me. It's possible that the strong winds outside made the house sway in such a way to cause the fall, or perhaps someone was trying to communicate with me in a purposeful way.

Shock filled my body. I was already unsettled by the storm, and the picture falling down in front of me really frightened me on some level. On another level, I was calmed by something familiar, a sense of my maternal grandfather, Grandpa Pat. It brought back fond memories of spending time with him when I was little in Indiana, near his house, catching fireflies and fishing. I didn't get to see him often, yet I remembered him as having always made me feel calm and deeply loved. I remember how excited I was when I was five and I learned he was coming to live with us, only to be crushed when I learned he was very sick. He passed away when I was six. Now, it seemed like he was trying to get my attention, but I didn't understand how, and while I was able to feel his calming presence, the face I saw in my mind didn't match that of the man I knew.

After several hours, the storm passed and I was able to relax and fall asleep. That night I had a dream, but it felt so real, it was as if I were wide awake. Grandpa

Pat told me he had come to take Mom with him, that it was time for her to go. The next morning, I talked to one of my sisters and found out she had also had a dream about Mom and death. I started to feel as if the time when Mom would pass from this physical life was near. My mind continued to want to control my circumstances, but the letting go I had been practicing was serving me well as I continued trying to trust the bigger picture called life and trusting that what came forth was what I could handle, and that I would always have everything I needed. I was choosing my faith story more and more as the days progressed.

Despite my practice of letting go, the sadness started to catch up with me. I was not ready to say goodbye, especially because I was finally experiencing the relationship with my mom that I had always wanted, one in which I felt her deep love and in which I knew she felt mine. Also, my sisters and I were in the planning stages of a big birthday celebration for Mom in March at that time, and I knew she would not be around much beyond that. Her body was showing signs of fatigue. Her blood pressure had been irruptive as of late and had shot up to 180 as her heart rate escalated.

These symptoms also reminded my father that this time was different for her, and that Mom might not be around much longer. He opened up to my sister that he didn't know what he would do without Mom. He said, "How in the world can I prepare for letting the love of my life go after fifty-five years of marriage?" He also struggled with wondering how his daughters would help themselves at the same time. I am not sure we knew at that point and definitely did not discuss it much, yet each of us seemed to be moving toward a place of acceptance, in our own way and on our own path.

The next week, in late January, I went to Austin to be with Mom, wanting to enjoy her time left on this earth, however long it lasted. Our visit was precious and lovely, difficult and tearful at the same time. I also had a chance to visit with my dear friend Corinne, who lived in Austin. She had lost her mother as a young child and was able to support me from a place of empathy, which felt different and deeply comforting. Corinne was my calm in the storm, a safe haven away from my family where I could start to feel the deep loss I was experiencing. She always knew what I needed and met me wherever I was emotionally with a heart full of compassion.

As we talked about the reality of my situation, she thought of things that might be helpful to Mom. What she remembered about her own mother's passing was how it would have been nice to have a piece of her mother's clothing, maybe multiple pieces, that she could make into a quilt and wrap around her. Something physical to comfort her and bring her close to her mother again in times of need. As I processed her kind advice, I knew it was valuable, yet I was not sure I was ready to internalize it, so I neatly tucked away her ideas in my memory for a later time.

꩜

As I moved into February, I was in a state of limbo. I was kind of numb, moving through my days without much feeling, as if I had moved back into my detached state as the sadness and pain in my heart were increasing. Once again, similar to a time in my not-so-distant past, I felt as if my life were leading me, not the other way around. I was also distracted by finishing the planning for Mom's birthday celebration with my sisters, now only a few weeks away.

I was jolted back to reality when the doctor delivered some more news that confirmed what I felt in my heart. He told us it was time for us to think about hospice for Mom. And then he said something more, put words out there that made her situation very real and short-term all of a sudden. He said, "My thoughts and prayers are with you as you endure this time"—the time before Mom would no longer be with us.

Chapter 8:

Time Slipping Away

*Faith is the daring of the soul to go farther
than it can see.*
—William Newton Clarke

As I thought about how my time with Mom was running out, I considered what I would do if I really did know she was close to passing. I struggled daily to keep a clear head and to focus on my deep love for her in the midst of these questions, yet fear kept creeping into my thoughts. As a way to maintain my faith and calm my soul, I often closed my eyes and took several deep belly breaths, inhaling the warmth of the precious and valuable love we shared—a love that had always been there but that I just hadn't allowed myself to feel until the past several years.

As I continued to breathe in and out, focusing on the love, I asked for answers about what I would do if she had only a month left with us. One idea that surfaced was that I would want something representative of Mom in my home, something more than a photograph in a frame. Something created from her heart. Mom had become quite a talented watercolor painter since she had retired twenty years earlier. As I continued to focus on this great talent of hers, I realized having something painted by her in our home would feel special. I wanted it to be a purposeful picture, one of a place we had been together. A painting for me, for my son, and for my daughter.

I called Mom and said, "I was just thinking of you and what an amazing artist you have become. The kids and I would really enjoy having some of your artwork in our home. We were thinking it might be fun to have some paintings of trips we've taken together. What do you think?"

Mom was thrilled. She said, "Yes, I would really enjoy painting some pictures for each of you. Do you remember the time your dad and I came with you to Sunset Beach in North Carolina when James was little? I really enjoyed the peaceful feeling of that beach." We also reminisced about being in Monterey, California, and visiting the aquarium, then walking along the ocean and seeing sea otters playing in the seaweed. Even in the midst of her deteriorating health state, Mom seemed to gain energy talking about different paintings she could make, wanting each to be unique and special for each of us.

In mid-February, I was scheduled to go on a business trip, when I learned Mom's blood pressure had been extremely high over the previous few days and was not going down. San Diego was my planned destination and sounded delightful at that time of year, a place to enjoy the sun's warmth and feel calmed by ocean waves. However, as I tried to complete my travel plans, I had a hard time, and my mind kept drifting back to Mom. I knew I wanted to go see her instead. I sat with my feeling of wanting to be by her side, as she had done so many times for me. I knew she was scared that her body was changing often and becoming more unpredictable. In that moment, I reminded myself of the short amount of time we had left together. I realized that work could wait this time and canceled my San Diego trip.

I did not discuss my change in plans with Mom and thought she would appreciate my showing up for a visit in Austin, unannounced. Wow, was I wrong. When I arrived to surprise her, she said, "Rebecca, it makes me really uncomfortable that you would do this. I'm worried about your job; I know it's been tough for you in the midst of all these changes. Are you sure this is okay?"

"Yes, Mom," I said. "I was able to have one of my team members go to San Diego instead. Work seems insignificant to me right now, when you're here experiencing different things in your body. I would not have been able to focus, and choosing to spend time with you instead really comforts me and brings me joy."

When I probed more about why she was uncomfortable, she said that it was hard for her to receive the gift of my visit, knowing that I had prioritized her over work. She had never wanted anyone to go out of their way for her, and she knew how important work was to me in my new head-of-household status. I wrapped my arms around her and reassured her that she was worthy of such a gift of love, especially knowing that our time together was slipping away. At that point, I had grown to rely more on my feelings versus my thoughts, the responsible side of me. As the little voice inside my gut telling me Mom's time was coming to an end gained strength, most everything seemed less important than enjoying time with her. In turn, she grew more comfortable with my choice as the day progressed.

While I was in Austin, I called Mom's doctor and learned that her high and erratic blood pressure was linked to her kidneys not working properly. Her doctor recommended that Mom see a renal specialist. As I processed his words, I remembered something a physician friend of mine had told me a while back when Mom had first been sick: that the renal system was usually the first to shut down, and sometimes that reality led to mandatory hospitalization of the patient.

I sat quietly as I absorbed this information and then called Mom's doctor again to ask him more questions about her recent test results and how they compared to previous months' results. Cancer markers were one way her doctor tracked the progression of the cancer, and he shared that Mom's cancer markers were now 6.1, out of a range of 0 to 3, when they had been just 1.5 three months earlier. A 6.1 cancer marker represented a rapid acceleration of the disease. Mom's doctor also shared that her lung tumor had tripled in size in the past few months. All of these facts about her health status were proof of my feelings that she would not be with us much longer. I felt a lump growing in my throat as I quietly thanked him and said goodbye.

As I hung up the phone, I felt paralyzed and numb. While what I probably needed most was a walk outside to clear my head, my energy levels felt zapped all of a sudden, and I didn't even feel strong enough to walk across the room. As I sat down and closed my eyes, thinking of the details I had just received, I reflected on how far I had come in the previous two years in terms of being willing to open my heart, be present in the moment, and allow myself to truly take in deep love. But now the pain I felt as new details revealed themselves one by one was so raw that I wasn't sure how to cope or what to do next.

As my pain radiated through me, I decided to focus on learning even more from Mom to continue to feel connected to her. I sat and talked with her and tried to fill in more missing details in the story of her life. It was a welcome distraction at the time, but once I returned home a few days later, I had a hard time focusing. I could barely carry out the basic tasks of my day and started forgetting things. The raw pain remained in my chest. I went to my therapist, seeking tools to help me cope. Trisha was a registered nurse and had advanced certifications in healing-touch therapies. She asked me to update her on Mom's situation.

"Mom's health is deteriorating very rapidly now," I said. "Her cancer markers have quadrupled in the past few months and are twice as high as the usual top range. Her blood pressure is very erratic, and her doctor said it's because her kidneys aren't working properly. I feel like everything is changing so quickly, and I'm really not ready to say goodbye to her. I'm feeling the pain so deeply in my heart, it's hard to breathe sometimes."

As I spoke, tears poured down my cheeks. The pain in my chest became more intense, and I started to feel chills up and down my chest and stomach. Trisha wrapped a blanket over me and responded, "Rebecca, I really admire you for choosing to allow your love for her to guide this journey as you prepare to say goodbye to her. The reality is that as you have allowed your heart to open so widely to feel deep love, you are feeling your pain on the same deep level."

Ouch. Ouch. Ouch.

During this visit, I asked for some helpful tools to allow release of this pain so it would not harm my body. Trisha recommended I start taking hot baths with two cups of Epsom salts a few times a week. She also recommended I buy three types of polished crystals to use directly on my body: amethyst, aquamarine, and rose quartz. Either I could lie down on my bed and place the crystals on my throat, heart, and just above my stomach, or I could put them in the bath with me. I chose the latter; the water felt so calming to me that I could actually drift off as I relaxed and let go. When I would lay on my bed with the crystals on my body, I also felt calm. I would move different stones to my throat or heart, depending on what felt most helpful. I put all three on my heart at once when the pain was most debilitating. As I put these tools to work, I also chose to focus on the gift of feeling deep love to enable me to make it through my days, one at a time.

As I was facing the reality of my mother dying, I was also approaching another court appearance related to my ex-husband and our separation. It was definitely not a pleasant experience, yet evidently the courts required it in order for our separation agreements to be accepted in Tennessee, after my move to Nashville. I was feeling very weak and not sure I could endure the emotion and stress of the courtroom. Anger rose up in my throat as I pondered having to face such impactful life experiences at the same time, once again.

Although it felt unfair and was more than I thought I could handle, the silver lining was that I realized that I had reached a place of community in my life in Nashville, a sense of belonging that meant I did not have to face this experience alone. I had developed great friendships and had family to support me. And at the core of my being, I also had my faith.

As I considered my support options, I thought back to several seemingly insurmountable experiences from my past where my faith had led me through my pain and darkness to peace and light. One was my divorce and separating my assets from my former husband's as my mother was first diagnosed with cancer. Another was learning of my mother's cancer metastasizing as I faced being laid off from my job. I closed my eyes and allowed for the release of these emotionally charged experiences, acknowledging in that moment that I really must be strong enough to overcome them, as God gives us only what we can handle. I had truly begun to believe in my own strength, even as my mom's life on Earth came to an end.

Chapter 9:

A Celebration of Love

With the new day comes new strength and new thoughts.
—Eleanor Roosevelt

As I prepared to be in Austin for Mom's seventy-seventh birthday, on March 9, I grew more depressed yet excited at the same time. In my daily calls with Mom, I started to notice her coughing more, and that part put me in a funk. The exciting part was that

Mom had survived long enough to be able to enjoy time with all of her daughters, her sons-in-law, her grandchildren, and one granddaughter-in-law in Austin as we came together to celebrate her. My godfather and his son were able to come as well. It was probably the most enjoyable family gathering I had ever experienced.

My children and I, and the rest of the family, all arrived at different times on Thursday, the day before, and spent time out at Mom and Dad's house on Lake Austin, sitting on the boat dock and telling stories from our childhood. On Friday, Mom's actual birthday, Dad rented a paddlewheel boat for all of us. We spent several hours out on Lake Austin, enjoying the sunshine, relaxing, and honoring Mom. I could tell by her expressions that it was hard for her to receive all the love that we had gathered just for her. She was still not used to the spotlight and continued to feel more comfortable in the background of these kinds of situations. I also noticed she had become much more visibly out of energy and more introspective than she had been even a few weeks prior. All the attention seemed to tire her out.

When we returned to the house after the boat ride, I offered to give Mom a foot massage, something that we were all starting to do more and more as our options to show how much we cared for her diminished along with her deteriorating health. She had us use her favorite Trader Joe's moisturizing lotion, which soaked into her feet quickly and was not greasy. These foot massages seemed to be one thing she was able to feel deeply and receive openly.

During that trip to Austin, I was also able to talk a little to my dad. I said, "It seems like it's becoming harder for you to watch Mom's energy decrease and her health deteriorate. I can see the surprise on your face when she's not able to walk like she used to. Would it be helpful to talk about how it feels?"

Tears filled his eyes as he heard my words, and he said, "Rebecca, I just love your mother so deeply. It's so hard to watch her change so quickly, and it makes me sad that she doesn't have the energy to walk much anymore. She is absolutely the love of my life. I knew that from the first moment I met her. She is also the most giving person I have ever met, always doing things for everyone else."

I wrapped my arm around his shoulder as he continued, "And would you please help make sure I am never put in a hospital after Mom dies? I want to be left right here."I comforted him and assured him that I would make sure his wishes were fulfilled. We were then able to talk about Mom's need for hospice, and he agreed that he should talk to Mom about it. Then he said, "Rebecca, you know that will be hard. Your mother and I don't really communicate very well, but I will definitely try to talk to her and explain how we need the help of hospice now."

Saturday, the day after Mom's birthday, Jim Innes, a family friend and accomplished photographer, came out to the lake to take family pictures. It was a little complicated trying to work with a group of fifteen people, many of us strong-willed and very particular about how we looked, but Jim was just the right person to make us laugh while capturing poignant moments.

Family photos were usually not a fond memory for any of us. When we were growing up, we all endured yearly trips to Olan Mills. In a family with five little girls, getting each one of us dressed appropriately was sometimes stressful, especially since Dad always wanted us to wear dresses and have our hair combed. Also, several of my sisters really did not like having their picture taken, period, on any occasion. Yet on this day we all surrendered and participated, knowing we would have some lasting memories documenting this celebration of love.

The next day, as we were packing our things to prepare to depart, Dad shocked us with a request that cast an even sharper dose of reality of the fact that Mom would be leaving us soon. He asked my sisters and me to gather together in the living room, out of Mom's earshot, and said, "Girls, it has been so amazing having each of you and your families here with us. I don't think we have every enjoyed each other more. That is what Mom wanted most, and we all were able to give it to her. Thank you all so very much."

He stopped for a moment and put his face in his hand as tears filled his eyes. He looked back up at us and said, "I need each of you to do something for me now. I would like each of you to write an obituary so we are prepared for when Mom takes her last breath. We don't really know how much more time we have with her, yet we can see her energy levels continue to drop."

We formed into a group hug around Dad as he started to cry out loud. My sense was that each of us held back our own tears to be strong for him, but his request left a sinking feeling in my stomach as I headed to the airport. I really did not want to leave. I was not sure I would see Mom alive again.

The next day, back at home, I learned that Mom

had a rough night after we left, with lots of coughing and difficulty breathing. One of my sisters, who
had stayed behind for a few more days with Mom,
called me that night to share some things she learned.
"Rebecca, Mom was happy beyond words that we all
came to visit. She told me that she was not sure she
would make it to her seventy-seventh birthday when
we started planning it in January. She was really surprised and delighted that she stayed alive. But what she
shared next was a little scary. She said that she felt like
it was okay to let go."

Carol and I cried for a few moments, knowing what
that meant. I thanked her for sharing, told her I loved
her, and hung up. As I sat there after the call, I felt panic
fill my body as the sense of time slipping away gained
momentum in my mind. All sorts of thoughts and feelings rushed through me as I attempted to process what
I was feeling. I deeply wanted to move to Austin for a
short time, to be with Mom and cherish each day she
had left. I allowed myself to dream of that possibility for
a moment as I pictured her in my mind. The concept was
a lovely thought, yet it conflicted with my reality. I knew
that my priority was raising two children back in Nashville, working full-time, and being the sole provider for
my children. Moving to Austin was not an option for me.
As my scattered thoughts started to hone in on the conflict I felt between wanting one thing and knowing my
responsibilities would not allow it, the racing in my mind
turned to fear of what was next. I was so very torn inside.

I closed my eyes and prayed for guidance. I knew if I
surrendered my situation to God, I would get answers—
maybe not right away or in the way I imagined, yet I

believed they would be for the best. So I asked for help and trusted that the details of my busy life would work out the way they needed to while I spent more time with Mom. And my prayers were answered: I was able to go back to Austin the very next weekend, for St. Patrick's Day, as were my two sisters who lived out of town. One thing that Mom had always loved was celebrating every holiday each year with special decor and foods. She always give us something small to signify each celebration, such as kitchen towels or napkins, and had continued that tradition even after we left home and were living on our own. In Austin, St. Patrick's Day was a nice distraction from what we all felt as Mom's health deteriorated at a rapid pace. We sat around the dinner table and took turns recounting stories of growing up in Houston. We laughed and cried together and deepened our connection as a family at the same time. Each of us was coping in our own way, and these experiences gave us comfort in the midst of our pain.

On that trip to Austin, I talked more with Mom about what she was experiencing day-to-day, what her life was feeling like now. She said, "Rebecca, I kind of feel lost these days, like I don't have a rudder to guide my life. I used to have such powerful energy inside me, and that kept me going each day. That feeling is gone now, and it's strange. I'm also having trouble being able to feel all of your love for me."

I held her hand and said, "Mom, I imagine that is such a different, difficult feeling for someone like you, who has always exuded energy. What kinds of things are you thinking about?"

She replied, "Oh, it's all negative self-talk. My

inner critic keeps asking why I can't just get up—as if it's that easy." Mom was not able to walk much on her own these days. And her appetite had diminished to virtually nothing. She went on, "Rebecca, do you think my lack of appetite and my inability to walk on my own are signs of the cancer spreading through my body, or are those things happening because I have such high blood pressure?"

That was a direct question I was not really ready for, but I took a deep breath and responded, "I'm not sure we really know, Mom. Since you've stopped seeing your doctor, he isn't able to tell us. It could be both."

She looked at me and said matter-of-factly, "You know, Rebecca, if it's my time to go, I accept it. I definitely don't want it to drag out or to be a burden on any of you girls."

I wrapped my arms around her and held her for a while. We both acknowledged that we didn't really know how or when it would happen, though I still remembered my dream that she would die in her sleep.

As I looked into her eyes while we talked, I saw a lightness I had never glimpsed before—an almost angelic light, shining brightly. She closed her eyes and drifted off as I held her arm. Her body was cold to the touch these days, almost as if it were empty.

The next time she opened her eyes, she talked about her acupuncture, which she had enjoyed weekly for over a year. Mom described how she was not able to relax enough now to receive the treatment. She knew she wouldn't reap the benefits if she were not able to relax, and she thought maybe her inability to do so stemmed from fear, or maybe she was afraid to let go, as it might mean letting go forever. She also told me how hard it was for her to lie in her bed and do nothing every day. Mom was used to a highly active state of being and not very comfortable sitting still, just being.

As I processed her words, I felt as if sadness were flowing through my veins and poisoning my spirit. But I gathered my strength and said, "Mom, I admire you for being so strong and accepting where you are in this moment. As hard as it is for me to say, I accept where you are at this juncture, and if your path is to leave, I am coming to terms with it."

She smiled and said, "Thank you, Rebecca. That means a lot to me. How will you remember me after I have died?"

Another sharp pain shot through my chest, and chills filled my body. I was grateful to be talking so openly with her, yet my heart was breaking into pieces as I took in her words.

Mom held my hand and said, "Rebecca, please don't remember me as I am today. I feel so weak and empty."

"Oh, Mom, definitely not," I reassured her. "I will remember the incredible gift you have given me, of sharing our deep love for each other so openly, the unending giving and incredible support you have always provided me, and the valuable guidance you have shared as a mother about how to raise children from one stage to the next."

Mom's eyes lit up. "Rebecca, I am so very lucky that you have included me in so much of your life. When you call me, I can almost feel your presence. It calms my mind and gives me peace. Thank you." I had started calling her daily by that point, and each time I did, I would visualize wrapping my arms around her. It was such great validation for me to hear her say this, as it was symbolic of our deep connection that could transcend geographic distances.

Mom drifted off again, and when she reopened her eyes, she said she knew how much I loved her. I paused and closed my own eyes for a moment. Here was more validation, giving me comfort. It felt as if this talk gave both of us strength. As if we were in our own little world having this discussion, while the busyness of everyone in the house moved around us.

As I prepared to leave again at the end of the weekend, my sisters and I were figuring out how to communicate better and talked about Mom's death in a little more straightforward, open way. Dad was, understandably, very sad and depressed. When I went to say goodbye to him, I hugged him for what seemed like hours while he surrendered to a deep belly cry. He said, "Rebecca, she is my rock, my everything. I was so sure she would survive this just like she did before. All of a sudden, this situation seems different, like she's not going to pull through and survive this time. I just don't know what I'm going to do without her." His words were muffled as the tears continued to pour from his eyes.

"Oh, Daddy, I know," I said. "I imagine words are not worthy of describing how deep a bond you two have created over five decades of marriage. I just want you to know I'm here and I love you." I gave him one last hug and said goodbye.

The day after I returned from Austin felt like a gift. It was a break from all the emotion and stress of the past couple of weeks. In some ways, I felt as if I were standing in the eye of a hurricane. My mind was calm and clear. I felt joy again and had a spring in my step. I also could feel the love and support from my dear friends. As such, I was able to focus and knock out a couple of items on my to-do list, a helpful change from the limbo I had been living in for the previous several weeks. I cherished the feeling that all was right in my world and my new normal was soothing and serene, at least for a moment in time. I enjoyed this feeling of peace and calm while it lasted.

My respite from grief lasted two days and was a much-needed break, especially for my body. My sadness had been manifesting itself in my body in the form of headaches, nausea, and leg cramps. I found it interesting that my two good days coincided with two good days for Mom. She was upbeat and in good spirits when I talked to her. Funny how connected our bodies can become with those of our loved ones.

The next day, my tears were back, welling up in my eyes and then pouring down my cheeks. Mom's two days of feeling good changed quickly. All of a sudden, her sodium levels were dangerously low and her blood pressure was still erratic and high. I called her to check in and said, "Mom, I heard you're back in bed. How are you feeling?"

"Oh yes, once again, Rebecca. My headaches are back, and I'm having muscle spasms up and down my legs." As we talked, Mom continued, "I am so amazed by watching you handle all you have been through and still keep such a positive attitude. You are such a gift to your children and me." Her comment caught me off guard, probably because I was so focused on her while she was still putting others first. I found it difficult to express in words my experience and why I chose to be positive, in part because the choice was a somewhat unconscious decision, based on my sense of responsibility for my children.

As we talked further, I realized that I had merely made a choice to face the pain and live through it, to move forward one step at a time. I had other choices, for sure: masking the pain or going crazy. Maybe it was my two children who depended on me for strength and guidance that kept me going and led me to this choice. Maybe my growing ability to trust my faith was also a reason, that feeling I had in my soul that even when I could not see through the fog, I felt strongly in my heart that whatever was happening was all for me. I just had to be patient sometimes in order for clarity to reveal itself.

At the end of March, Mom decided to stop taking her blood pressure medicine, since it was not working. And, once again, she had strength. She was able to go outside and walk down the street, to the big tree in the middle of the road, about three houses away. Dad was convinced she had "turned the corner." I was supportive of his positive outlook even while I felt this tug inside—kind of like a yo-yo. Mom experienced really good days and really tough, low days. The roller coaster continued to change direction quickly, and the emotions followed suit. The low days always came back with a vengeance.

By April 1, her headaches had increased so much and her sodium levels had dropped so low that Dad became very worried and took her to the emergency room. When the ER doctor came in to see her, Mom told him she was "not supposed to be here." She explained that she felt like she "should already be dead" and that something was keeping her here. It was probably shocking for the doctor to hear and even more so for Dad.

Mom spent the day in the emergency room while they stabilized her with fluids, as she would not let them run any tests. We did learn from this ER doctor that the lung tumors were likely depleting the sodium in her body and might eventually cause a heart attack. When she told me about the experience later, Mom said she was consciously focused on trying to shut down the organs in her body, as she really didn't want to live in the state she was in any longer. She was done. Mom actually believed that her mind was strong enough to shut down her body. She never ceased to amaze me with her expansive beliefs. I listened intently yet didn't quite comprehend. I wanted to help her, but I didn't know how.

After the emergency room experience, Dad was finally able to convince Mom to let hospice come help. Mom wanted to stay at home, and hospice would enable her to feel more comfortable and manage her pain better. While I had known this phase was coming, it was shocking nonetheless. The pain in my chest spread far and deep, sending fever-like chills through my arms and legs. I knew it was time to take my children to see her to say goodbye in person.

My kids and I traveled to Austin in early April to celebrate the love we shared with Mom. As I thought about how her health might be inhibiting her normal routine, I realized that in her current, frail state, she was not able to walk down to the lake anymore. Mom had followed Dad to several different cities and states during their marriage, and so they had agreed that she would get to pick where they retired. Her choice had been to retire on a lake.

As I reflected on her decision, a thought popped into my head. Since she was not able to go down to the lake anymore, maybe I could take the lake to her. *Really?* I asked myself. *Well, sort of.* I took a plastic tub down to the lake's edge and filled the tub with water, sand, and shells. The added contents made the tub quite heavy, but I was determined to complete this process, so I carried it back up the hundreds of stairs to the house. I am not sure how I managed to do that, maybe adrenaline, but something definitely gave me strength, even though I had to stop every half dozen steps, put down the bucket, and wipe the beads of sweat from my forehead. Each time I stopped to rest, I imagined the joy on Mom's face as she felt her toes in the sand and the water. That feeling gave me more energy, and I would conquer a few more steps. I think my sisters thought I had lost my mind.

When I brought the tub inside the house to Mom, I set it down on the floor next to her bed. She opened her eyes and smiled when I said, "Mom, I brought you a special treat. Since you're not able to walk down to the water anymore, I brought some water and sand to you. Here, let me help you sit up so you can stick your toes in the bucket." I placed her feet in the water, one at a time.

Her eyes lit up brightly, and she seemed to exude peace as she said, "Oh, Rebecca, this is such a thoughtful gift. I kind of feel like I'm standing in a foot of water down at the lake. Thank you so much!" My heart expanded with joy at having been able to grant her this moment of peace and happiness, a break from the pain and suffering.

The intensity of the visit was definitely taking its toll on me, although I was trying to stay strong for Mom and for my children. I started to feel my well of grief trying to get my attention and take over my focus, and I knew I needed support outside of my family. I reached out to my friend Corinne and asked, "Hey, are you home right now? I really need a break for a moment."

She said, "Oh, yes, Rebecca. Come on over." It was so comforting for me to have her support, and it allowed me a safe space to let go a little, fall apart, and feel my deep pain for a short time, in a place where I didn't feel the need to be strong. We talked through the situation and the signs of the end approaching quickly. I was struggling to figure out how to help Mom feel loved every day, even though I could not be with her.

Because Mom was a believer in so many healing therapies, including the power of crystals, I got the idea, as Corinne and I talked, to make Mom a necklace, something she could wear every day to remind her of our deep love, even though we were many miles away. I asked Corinne to go on an errand with me, and she knew just where to take me. We ventured into the bead store, where I found what I was after. In the first glass case we came to, there was a deep-purple amethyst crystal and two smaller rose quartz crystals next to it. Those were Mom's favorite colors: pink and purple. It was almost as if they had been placed right there for me to see. I strung all three together on a pink piece of leather with the amethyst in the middle and the rose quartz on either side. I finished making the necklace and was delighted at the thought of surprising Mom when I returned to her side.

When I returned to the house, I went in to Mom's room. She had dozed off. I spoke her name gently, and she woke up and smiled when she saw me. "Mom, I have a surprise for you. Close your eyes for a moment." I walked over to her, leaned over her chest, and tied the necklace around her neck. I grabbed a mirror and told Mom to open her eyes. "Oh, Rebecca, this is so beautiful. And in my favorite colors. So sweet and thoughtful of you. Thank you," she said. As I looked at her face, her brightness was so radiant, it was as if her joy was beaming from deep inside her body, almost as if the light was shining straight out from her soul.

As we sat together, I could see Mom visibly relax. She closed her eyes yet still had a grin on her face. When she opened her eyes again, she shared how calming the necklace was, how she felt more settled with it on. We then moved on to a discussion about her remaining time on Earth being short. It reminded me that Dad had asked my sisters and me a few weeks prior to write an obituary for Mom. While the thought was deeply difficult on some level, I felt mostly prepared for her impending departure, as Mom had shared so much about her life in the preceding months. However, there was one more thing I still wanted to know, in her own words. I wanted to know how she wanted to be remembered, what she would say about her life. So I asked.

Mom replied that she "gave all the time and love," and that it was "so easy to give but so very hard to receive." I was thankful to have the time to ask her this question, and I was not surprised by her response.

As I reflected on the day, sitting with the feeling that I had brought the lake water to her room and made the necklace, a little gift from my heart—something she had selflessly given to me many times—filled me with peace. In that moment, I knew deep in my soul that my loving gifts had made a difference for her, and I was able to breathe a sigh of relief, knowing we had shared yet another celebration of our love for each other.

Chapter 10:

A Symbol of Connection

*Happiness is not found in things you
possess, but in what you have the courage
to release.*
—Nathaniel Hawthorne

While I felt very lucky to have the gift of time to say goodbye over a long period, it was quite a struggle to manage my grief and pain day by day. One of the tools I used for support and calm in the storm was getting regular massages to help my body release its sadness. When I visited Mom in Austin, I continued this practice and extended it to her. We would have someone come to Mom's house, and we would both enjoy the peace we felt following every treatment.

On my trip in April 2006, my discussion with the massage therapist took a slightly different turn down a path I was not expecting or even could have imagined. As Amy, the therapist, worked on releasing the tension in my muscles, she acknowledged how I was feeling, as she had lost her mother at age three. She said, "Rebecca, I can empathize with how scared you feel knowing your mother will die soon and not knowing what to do or how to prepare for such a deep loss. I lost my mother at a very young age. I still remember how sad I was every day without her. My sadness came out as anger some days, tears other days. I was desperate some days to feel connected to my mom. I felt closest to her outdoors in the woods or by a stream. I would grasp at the smallest symbol that might have represented my mom after she died."

She paused for a moment to work out a knot in my shoulder, then continued, "On one of my tougher days, when I was walking on a trail near our house with my father, I felt a surge of energy and joy when I saw a certain kind of rock that reminded me of her, thinking it represented my mom. Then I convinced myself that was just my mind making up stories and dismissed the thought. I wondered around feeling like I was in the dark for a long time after my mom died. I really struggled with how to find peace."

As she spoke, she started to make connections to

my situation and quickly transitioned to talk about my own mom, to whom she had given a massage before me. Amy said, "It really felt like your mom was different this time, like she is preparing to leave. Her body felt different also." She stopped and worked out another knot in my back. She said, "Rebecca, I really want your experience to be different from mine. I'm hoping this doesn't sound crazy to you, but I have learned as I have become an adult that it is possible to connect with loved ones after they die. You have a choice to create a lasting and true connection to your mom, if you are open to considering it."

I was pretty relaxed by this point yet still wanted to grasp onto anything I could to stay connected to Mom. I said, "I'm not sure I really understand what you're saying, although I'm interested to learn more. What do you mean, exactly?"

Amy responded, "I would recommend talking with your mom and explaining my story. Let her know that you want to work with her to define a special symbol of connection. The symbol needs to be something so unique to the two of you that you will not question it once you see it, like I did with the rock."

In the midst of my grief and pain, this concept felt like a glimmer of hope on one hand and far-reaching on the other. I still didn't fully grasp what she was saying or what it meant at the time, but later that day, the thought of having a lasting connection with Mom kept popping into my mind. Every time it did, I felt joy and peace. Something was guiding me forward to take the next step. Maybe it was an extension of believing in something magical, as I did when I was a child, like

Santa Claus or the Easter Bunny, that led me down a path to want to learn more and to bring it up with Mom. That comparison to something childlike and magical helped me feel in my heart that it was okay, that I was not crazy, to want to pursue such a thought.

The idea stuck with me and continued to gain traction, so I decided to ask Mom. I shared Amy's advice and told Mom the story of when Amy lost her mom and how she struggled to connect. When Mom said she was open to hearing more, exploring the idea further, and creating a symbol, she gave me more positive reinforcement to continue down this path. Mom wanted to figure out together with me what that symbol might be, so that when she connected from heaven, I could be sure it was her. We talked about how to make such a decision, how to pick something that was unique enough that I would not question it yet clear enough that in the moments when it revealed itself, I would feel her love.

Mom wanted me to bring her some suggestions. She didn't feel as if she was thinking clearly these days. She asked me to go down to the lake, stand in the water, and stare across to the other side. She said I should clear my mind and allow the answer to come forward. As a people-pleasing type of person by nature, I felt compelled to follow her direction. Although I was still not sure what I was heading off to do, it was probably my desire to continue my deep connection with Mom after she passed that pushed me forward on this journey. So off I went.

I walked down to the lake, waded out into the water about knee deep, and gazed across to the other side of the lake, taking in the beautiful view. I looked around me, watching the waves as they washed to the shore around my knees and crashed up against the limestone retaining wall behind me. I looked up at the trees and watched the leaves sway in the breeze. I looked back across the lake and saw a dragonfly with purple wings fly by, then land on a leaf nearby. I had come here many times, yet this time felt different. I felt especially calm and peaceful, and I sensed pure love around me, as if someone I loved was holding me.

I closed my eyes and asked God for an answer. *What kind of symbol of connection would be meaningful to both Mom and me?* I let go of the thought and waited patiently for a response. I kept my eyes closed. Surprisingly, the answer flowed into my mind quickly. Mom and I shared purple as a favorite color. Seeing the dragonfly with purple wings made me think of our favorite insects. The thought that popped in my mind was a purple butterfly, although I didn't understand it at the time. We both loved butterflies and used to enjoy going to butterfly museums. Dad had planted alyssum plants and butterfly bushes in the front yard to attract butterflies. And here I was with some kind of answer, even though I was not sure exactly what it meant or even that I trusted this process.

I thought of this concept over and over as the water rose and fell around my legs. This entire exercise was happening because I had made a choice to believe and push my edges beyond the black and white I knew, to the gray I was learning to embrace. I was willing to do almost anything to create a lasting connection with Mom, knowing she was dying. Amy had inspired me and given me hope, so I held on to the answer and decided to pursue it further.

I walked back up to the house, somewhat in a daze, thinking of this answer but not sure what to make of it. Mom was asleep, so I spent time playing with my children. When Mom woke up, I went in to share what had come to me. "Mom, I think I have an idea of a symbol. What do you think of a purple butterfly as our symbol of connection?"

Her eyes lit up, and she said, "Oh, Rebecca, a purple butterfly is perfect." She beamed as she considered this symbol of our connection—purple was our favorite color, and our favorite insect was a butterfly. Silently, I questioned how it could be perfect, since it was not even something that could be found in nature, and, as such, I felt a little strange agreeing to something so unique, since I was not sure I would ever see one. However, I decided to quiet my internal critic and sit with how this felt. I truly wanted to believe—what a blessing it would be if this could be real. When I chose to embrace this symbol, it was truly magical how quickly I experienced that purple butterflies *are* real in nature. I cherished this special moment with Mom as we co-created a symbolic connection that would last forever, across different realms.

As my visit in Austin with Mom drew to a close, I was able to sit with her one last time. She was much more withdrawn from what was going on around her now; she seemed focused mostly inward. Her speech was slurred some, and she coughed often. She was not able to walk on her own anymore and was sleeping more often during the day. I sat next to her and held her hand. Touch and space were more what we shared now. She looked up at me and smiled and then looked beyond my shoulder, as if there were someone there. I was puzzled when she did this, especially since she smiled in the process. I looked over my shoulder and saw nothing. "Mom," I said, "what are you looking at?"

She smiled and spoke softly, in a raspy voice: "Oh, it's my dad. He and Mom are here with me." Her parents had both passed when I was very young, so I was confused by what she meant, but my experiences were increasingly pushing me way beyond my safe boundaries of understanding now, and this was definitely one of those moments. So I decided to go with what Mom was saying and let go of my need to understand it.

Mom turned her attention back to me and spoke softly. She said, "Honey, the good news is that I finally feel at peace with myself, with all the people who are special to me, whom I love, and with my life. I feel like all my work here is complete."

"Oh, Mom," I said, "I'm so glad to hear that. It warms my heart to know you are at peace. Thank you for sharing."

Each of my children spent time talking to Mom one-on-one. It was so difficult for them to see her in bed and unable to walk on her own. The grandma they were used to running and jumping with was not the same. I could see tears in their eyes as they each came out of her room. Then we said goodbye to her—maybe until the next time, maybe forever.

Before I left the house, I went looking for the pamphlet that the hospice nurse had left. Hospice was a gift to us all at that time, as the organization and staff enabled Mom to stay in her own bed in her home, fulfilling her wishes. The nurses were gracious and caring. They wanted to make sure Mom was comfortable and that we each knew what would happen as the days passed.

This pamphlet explained the dying process, something I had never observed so closely before. Suddenly, I was more interested to read about what would happen, since my experiences with Mom were expanding my beliefs at an accelerating rate. As I read the pamphlet, I started to feel a little more normal, that maybe I was not losing my mind. I found a description of what I had just experienced with Mom and her parents in a passage that read: "disorientation: when close to dying, a person often becomes confused, may see and converse with loved ones who have died before them." On some level, I was fascinated by the intricacies of life and these details of the process of the physical life ending. On another level, my heart almost felt like it was on fire, radiating out in all directions, knowing that my goodbyes and hellos to Mom would be over soon.

Back home in Nashville the next day and beyond, I tried to move through my tasks and stay busy by focusing on my children's needs and on work, but I was mostly kidding myself. I would start one thing and then end up doing something totally different, almost as if I had "lost" a moment of time in the transition. Something that seemed to keep me somewhat focused was regular exercise, both in the gym and at the park on the trails. Even though Mom was not able to say much anymore and her speech was slurred when she did, I still called her every day. During these calls, I would mostly share what was going on in our lives. When I checked in on how she felt and what was important to her each day, sometimes I would get one word, sometimes I would hear only coughing on the other end of the line.

On one particular day when I called, I could feel her smile as she shared something that gave her joy. She said, in slurred speech, "Honey, you know how I'm not able to get out of bed on my own anymore?"

"Yes, Mom."

"Well, I feel very special today." She stopped and coughed for a minute. She then said, very softly and in a somewhat muffled voice, "The minister from church came by and delivered an Easter service to me. He said a special prayer of healing. Oh, he is so nice."

I said, "Oh, Mom, that is so thoughtful. You are deserving of his grace—you have given so much to your church. And, Mom, as much as I would like to come back and see you soon, I feel in my heart that it is more important for you and Dad to have time together alone now to cherish the deep love you share. I love you."

Mom agreed. Then she talked about her life and how she had spent it always going, going, going, rarely sitting still in a day, and often helping others. As she spoke, she was able to verbalize that now she could look back and see that she never really fully relaxed, ever. She said she never just sat around and read or painted, solely focused on what she had been doing in the moment. Instead, while she painted or read, she had always been thinking of something else at the same

time. Or she had interrupted her quiet time to go help
others in need. While it was difficult for her to say all
of that and some of it was hard to understand, Mom
ended by saying that while she had the time now to just
be still, it was still somewhat foreign to her and made
her uncomfortable.

❦

Several weeks went by. The heaviness in my chest was
becoming a permanent fixture, and the physical mani-
festations of my pain continued in the form of nausea
and cramping down my legs.

I did have a moment of peace and joy when I
heard what Mom shared one day. She sounded weak
and her speech was fuzzy, yet I could still understand
her words as she said, "You know what, Rebecca? The
brightest part of my day now is when Dad rubs my feet
with the lotion Carol got from Trader Joe's before we
go to bed each night."

It was such incredible validation for me of the choice
I had made, to create space for Mom and Dad to share
their deep love in these last weeks and days. I could sense
Mom's joy when she spoke of Dad rubbing her feet, and
I knew she was able to actually feel his enduring love for
her. It made me smile and gave me comfort.

Right before we hung up, Mom said, "And you
know what else?" She stopped talking for a minute
to cough then continued, "I feel totally full of peace
now. You know those negative voices I told you I used
to hear in my head, telling me I wasn't good enough?

Well, all of those thoughts are gone now. I no longer hear them. My mind is quiet and I am relaxed. I am so glad. I love you so very much, Rebecca!"

I could tell all the talking had worn her out, so we said goodbye and hung up.

As Mother's Day approached, I decided I would spend it with my children and then go to Austin a few days later, in time for my dad's birthday. I was torn between supporting my children and being with Mom. I was also still trying to keep a semblance of focus on work and was expected to be in Monterey for an important leadership event the day after Mother's Day. It was my company's annual strategic leadership summit and a first for me in my new role. I had been looking forward to this event since I had been promoted, but I had mixed feelings as I boarded a plane headed west at 7:00 P.M. on Mother's Day.

When I landed in California around 10:00 P.M., I felt in my heart that I would not be there long. I tossed and turned most of that night, trying to relax, but my mind raced, wondering why I felt that way. After talking with one of my sisters the next morning, I learned why. Evidently, Dad had shared something openly during Mother's Day brunch. He had told Mom in front of my sisters that she was the love of his life, and that while he wanted to spend the rest of his life with her, he knew it was time for her to go and that she could leave with his deep love and full blessing.

As I listened to the words from my sister on the phone, I thought about how it was touching for Dad to have shared his feelings so openly, and in front of others. I was also amazed that he had the courage and strength to set Mom free and allow for her to transition with love. Chills ran up and down my spine as I processed this information. I felt deeply peaceful and heartbroken at the same time as I considered how that moment must have felt to Dad, Mom, and my sisters who had been there.

I sat still with all of these feelings for a minute, and then I remembered something else I had read in the hospice pamphlet: that sometimes people who are dying must wait until they are "released" by their loved ones before they can feel fully ready to pass on. Dad had just "released" Mom with those loving words, set her free so she could leave. Now it was time for me to drop everything and fly to Austin.

Chapter 11:

Transitions with Peace

*It is faith that steers us through stormy
seas, faith that moves mountains, and faith
that jumps across the ocean.*
—Mahatma Gandhi

My heart was heavy as I sat on the plane. I put
on my headphones to quiet the noise from the
engines and to signal to the people sitting near me to
give me space. Even though I knew the time was near,
it still felt like fresh news that my mom would be leaving us soon. Tears welled up in my eyes as I thought of
what I would find when I arrived, but focusing on the

deep love I shared with Mom helped me keep my composure. And I remembered our symbol again, delighted to have something unique to our connection.

When I arrived at my parents' house and saw Mom, she was quite weak. She slept most of the time during the day. She opened her eyes from time to time, but only for a few minutes. On May 18, my sisters and I celebrated our dad's eighty-second birthday with him while sitting on Mom's bed, including her in the celebration as best we could. We each did our best to celebrate while we knew the end was in sight. As Dad opened his gifts, he brought up fun memories of previous birthdays. We even took pictures willingly, although Mom was asleep during them. Her blood pressure was still quite low, and she had mostly stopped eating—two more signs, we had learned from hospice, that the dying process was accelerating and would end soon.

The next morning, Friday, I went into Mom's room and she seemed asleep. I sat with her one-on-one and cupped her hand in both of my hands. It was cold to the touch, even though she was covered with blankets and it was ninety-five degrees outside. I could almost hear her voice even when her eyes were closed and her lips were still. It was as if her soul were talking to me. I heard her say, *Rebecca, I am really scared to leave this physical world. I am not sure what will happen, what I will find when I leave, or how it will feel to transition. I wonder if I am worthy of receiving God.*

I was a little surprised to experience such a faithful woman having doubts about what would happen next and how the transition to heaven would happen. I sat quietly with her and closed my eyes.

What happened next was one of the most amazing and expansive experiences of my life, yet it also expanded my thinking beyond my threshold of understanding and belief. It was as if I were being given the gift of being a vessel to help Mom visit where she was headed next, to reassure her of the peace she would feel and that she was worthy of receiving God, and to help her embrace self-love completely.

The visual I saw next, with my eyes closed, was startling on the one hand and purely calming on the other. Somehow, Mom and I were all of a sudden standing on a beach, one of her favorite places to spend time. It felt similar to what I imagined the purest place on Earth would be like, a pristine setting with white sand stretching as far as we could see. I felt more whole and calm than I had at any other time I could remember. I could feel the sand between my toes and the water lapping at our feet as I held Mom's hand. The sun was shining brightly, and the sky was a vivid blue. Light beamed from Mom's eyes, expressing her joy about standing on the beach.

As I looked at her, I wondered what beach we were standing on. I was focused intently on Mom's reaction, wondering if she knew where we were, seemingly by ourselves. All of a sudden, I looked around us and realized we were not alone. There were fifty or more people standing on the beach with us, clothed in white and brilliantly illuminated from the inside out, shining brightly as if they were candles dancing in the wind— except there were no candles around us. The light was so bright, almost blinding to the naked eye, that I was not able to discern many details.

I had read about people's experiences with angels in books and had seen representations of angels in the movie *City of Angels* before, but I was surprised to realize I was not afraid at all. Mom did not seem afraid either. The glow in her eyes reflected the radiance around us. What I felt in my body was pure and expansive love in every cell of my being, as if I were radiating light myself.

In the Bible, Jesus speaks about the highest form of love being agape love—a type of love that gives life meaning and substance through voluntary sacrifice for the benefit of another person, without expecting anything in return. In this moment, I realized that I was feeling this type of selfless love, a source of absolute strength and power that could transcend time and physical space. As I looked at Mom, her facial muscles all relaxed and a smile began to emerge—a smile without any pain or regret or suffering, just pure light. Time seemed to be suspended as we stood there, taking in the beauty and grace of the light around us. We stood there for what seemed like hours yet could have been minutes. The only sound we could hear was the rush of waves crashing on the shore.

Then Mom spoke to me. "Rebecca, I feel so at peace. I am no longer afraid of where I am headed next. I feel like this place where we are is heaven. It is not scary at all. I feel comfortable letting go now and transitioning to heaven."

All of a sudden, the experience was over. I opened my eyes and was still sitting on her bed, holding her hand, in Austin, Texas, yet still feeling expansive love and light in every cell of my being.

I had seen experiences like this in movies and had read about people who had had experiences similar to what I had just saw and felt. One of the most memorable books I read on the subject was *The Shack*. The experience Paul Young describes in chapter 15, "The Festival of Friends," is very similar to my experience with Mom. He writes of having felt "larger than life, as if I were able to be present wherever I looked. . . . There were no candles—they themselves were lights."

I had been amazed at how calming reading about these kinds of encounters had felt yet had believed that very few people actually had these experiences. But for some reason, Mom chose me to help her in this moment one last time. Our mutual investment in developing a deep relationship over the previous several years enabled me to be open enough to receive this gift of love and light. As I took in the agape love, the expansive feeling of joy and grace continued to radiate through my body.

I wonder why she chose me, I thought. Maybe the process of opening my heart and allowing my faith to guide me over the previous three years had paved the way for me to open my mind enough to embrace this journey. What I was certain of was how grateful I was for that experience and the ability to provide one last gift to Mom, a gift of service to set her free. I knew then that it would be a matter of only hours or days until she transitioned. The signs were all there.

After that, it was time for me to go home, wrap my children in love, and support them as we faced what I knew was coming. I was torn about leaving, still not really wanting to say goodbye for good. But as hard as it was to leave, knowing I would not be there when she passed, in my heart I was at peace with my connection to Mom. I had practiced giving selflessly from my heart to her. I had had the gift of time to say all I wanted to say and to heal from the past, when I had not been able to receive Mom's love. I had transitioned from a stubborn little girl who did not know Mom's love growing up, no matter how thoughtful and giving she was, into a woman whose heart had expanded several times over and who now had a deep bond with Mom. And more than anything, I knew Mom would want me to go be with my children and nurture them when she passed. So I went to the airport and flew back to Nashville.

Once I got home, I was so distracted and sad that I found it difficult to focus on my kids. I knew they could probably sense my deep distress, but they were too young to be able to verbalize how that made them feel. Instead, their anger erupted in spurts, as they fought over toys or TV shows over that weekend.

On Sunday, May 21, I knew we needed to do something to keep our minds off things for a while and quell all the fighting, so we went to see the play *Annie* at the Tennessee Performing Arts Center. The music and dancing helped calm our nerves, and we were even able to laugh at times.

The very next day, early in the morning on May 22, I was awakened by the sound of pouring rain and loud thunder. I looked at my clock. It was 4:00 A.M. I had chosen to sleep upstairs in the guest room that night to be close to my children. Mom used to help them through storms by telling them that when it thundered, it meant the angels were bowling in heaven. And boy, were they loud on this Monday morning.

I sat there quietly in my bed, listening to the storm, and then I felt it—I felt Mom's physical life come to an end. It was almost as if I could hear her last breath. I lay still, thinking I knew what had just happened yet not entirely sure. I listened to the rain pouring down, watched the lightning flash across my room, and heard the thunder reverberating through the house.

At 4:30 A.M., the phone rang. It was one of my sisters. She had awakened as well and had gone in to Mom's room right as she took her last breath. I stayed on the phone and spoke with each of my sisters and my father for about an hour, feeling the peace that Mom's suffering was over. I felt as if I were in the room, transcending thousands of miles, and very connected to each of them and to Mom. While it was a deeply sad moment for each of us, we had developed a unifying bond over the past year, and that was a great blessing in the midst of our loss. And our opportunity to say goodbye over a long period of time felt like a gift of grace.

A waterfall of tears began flowing down my face, in part a selfish reaction to my loss, in part tears of pure joy for the depth of love I had been able to share with Mom and for my closeness with my family.

A few hours later, my children and I gathered our things to fly to Austin. As prepared as I had been, I was still in shock and quite distracted and out of sorts. As I tried to prepare us to leave, my dear friend Lyn came over to help us pack and get organized. She had been on standby to help and proved herself to be a giving and supportive friend.

We made it to the airport, and I called the school to let them know the children would be out for a few days. Something gave me strength to keep my composure for my children as we shared stories of Grandma on our flight. We remembered the first time she showed my son how to make a snowman, when he was one year old, in Boulder. Since I had grown up in Houston, it was not a skill I had learned. I think we had one dusting of light snow one Christmas growing up.

My daughter remembered how Mom had intervened when her brother took a toy from her hands. Mom had picked my daughter up and said she had something better. She put my daughter down near the attic stairs and said she would be right back. Mom came back down the stairs with a Catwoman doll on a motorcycle. She handed it to my daughter and said, "Sharing is always nice, yet having your own is sometimes a good thing."

My son decided to write a note to her and capture some of his memories. We had so many wonderful stories to share that the time on the flight went by very quickly.

When we arrived at Mom's house, she was still lying in her bed, as if she were sleeping. She looked peaceful and beautiful, and the skin on her face was taut, with almost no wrinkles. One of my sisters took my children down to the lake to build a sandcastle, giving me time alone with Mom. I sat on the side of the bed and said a prayer for her peaceful transition. As I sat there quietly, I could feel her presence strongly, as if she were still there. I sat there in the stillness for some time and said my last goodbye.

Mom's minister came over about an hour later to perform a service with all of us in the room. He asked us to hold hands. My son read the note he had written on the plane about all Mom had taught him, and my daughter went over and kissed Mom's face and touched her arm. I was stunned by the strength and comfort of my babies in this moment, as they did not seem afraid in the least. A feeling of pure love surrounded us all as the minister spoke. "I hope you all know how much your mother gave to the church, as a Stephen minister and in so many other ways. I know you are proud of all she gave, and seemingly so effortlessly." And then he smiled and shared something new. "The one thing I will remember most about Marj is how she could embrace her traditional Christian faith and faithfully listen to my sermons every Sunday, yet she would then come up to me later and challenge me to expand my beliefs further, beyond traditional Methodist ideas." He talked about how she had studied and embraced other religions and had wanted her pastor to integrate some of those concepts into his talks, but she had always made those requests in a calming way, he said.

We all smiled as tears streamed down our faces. While I was not aware that Mom had done this, it sounded like something she would do. She had shared new concepts with me when appropriate situations arose, and here I was, learning she had done the same with him. That was my mother, always wanting to share and grow.

Mom chose for her body to be cremated and wanted her ashes spread in all of her favorite places. After the lovely service in her room with our immediate family, we followed the hearse with her body in it to the place where she was to be cremated, supporting her safe passage. Mom had learned through her studies of Buddhism that Buddhists believed it took seven days for a soul to completely leave a body. As such, she had arranged with the funeral home to hold her body for seven days before completing the cremation. We learned of this prearranged agreement when Dad spoke with the funeral home to request a transport for her body. We were all still so numb from the shock and finality of her passing that it was difficult to process what that really meant. As the news sank in, it started to feel like a gift of time, a gift of compassion and grace. The seven days of waiting to complete the cremation process gave me time to grieve in my own way, as privately or in as supported a way as I chose. Even in her death, Mom was thoughtful and giving.

The weekend approaching was Memorial Day weekend. Since we had to wait, we decided to schedule the service on the Saturday following Memorial Day in order to give others time to arrange to join us. As my children and I flew home on Tuesday evening, I fought back tears and reflected on Mom's life, the incredible impact of one person and the lasting gifts she had bestowed on me and my children. And then I remembered the purple butterfly—our unique symbol of connection. I still had no tangible idea of what it really meant and felt a little strange thinking about it. Little did I know what I would experience next and how my edges would be pushed one more time, so very soon after her death.

Chapter 12:

Learning to Cope

There will come a time when you believe
everything is finished. That will be the
beginning.
—Louis L'Amour

When I was back home the next day, the reality of Mom's passing smacked me hard. A thick fog of grief engulfed me. I felt a pervasive pain in my upper body, so strong it seemed as if my chest were cut wide open, with a deep ravine carved through the middle. I got chills, as if my heart were pumping blood down this ravine. I struggled to make it through an hour without crying uncontrollably.

When I ventured out to feel normal, going to a grocery store I shopped at many times a week, I found myself paralyzed. I walked into the store with my list, only to feel like I didn't know where I was and not sure what to do. My legs felt as if they were immersed in quicksand suddenly, and I was unable to move. While it felt like an hour, it was probably only a couple of minutes. I was completely unaware of people around me or their expressions. Nothing seemed important anymore. Not even getting food to nourish my children.

The words my therapist had taught me for times like this eventually came back to me. As I started repeating to myself, *Right now I am taking one step in front of another*, I was able to move through the store and complete my shopping. When back at home, I walked around my house in a daze. I would start one task, only to end up focused on something else and unable to account for the time in between.

As I wandered around in this fog, I felt like I had been swept into a void. Gone were my daily calls with Mom and any means of helping me feel physically connected to her. I wanted most to touch her, wrap my arms around her, and hug her. I would pick up my phone some moments to call her, only to remember she had passed. I began to grasp for any physical representation that connected me to what she loved. Magnolias were one of her favorite flowers, and she always had cut ones in the house when they were in season, from the trees in our yard.

One day, feeling so lost that I could scarcely remember my own name, I walked into my backyard and wandered around, hoping the fresh air would help me. As I turned toward my neighbor's backyard, a flash of light caught my eye. It was a beautiful white flower blooming halfway down on a magnolia tree.

A spark of energy shot through my veins, and I turned back to my porch to pick up some clippers. I walked over and cut the magnolia off the tree, leaving several leaves on the stem, just as my mother had done countless times. As I walked back into the house, holding the stem, touching the roughness of the backside of the leaves, I felt close to Mom. I stopped and rubbed the leaves, closing my eyes and imagining Mom was standing next to me. It was silly, maybe, yet it calmed me and gave me peace in that split second—something I longed for every moment.

In an effort to get my body moving and to further distract myself, I loaded Carmella, my chocolate Lab, into the car and drove to the neighborhood park. Being outside provided an ounce of peace to my broken heart as I felt the wind swish around my arms. Carmella and I walked around the park loop a couple of times, fairly briskly. It felt kind of like I was in a hurry and running somewhere—I just wasn't sure where.

I saw several white butterflies fluttering near the trail as we completed each loop. On the fourth time walking around the loop, something caught my eye in one moment and was gone from sight the next. I walked closer to see if I could discern what it was. I sat still and waited for it to reappear. As if out of nowhere, there it was again, fluttering about three feet over the creek. Moving ever so quickly, I saw that it was clearly lavender in color, and almost iridescent. I stopped to watch this very special gift in hopes of seeing it land on something. It alighted on a leaf and disappeared almost instantly, virtually invisible to the naked eye.

I was shocked and speechless at what I was experiencing in this moment. It was a real purple butterfly— evidence that my mother was connecting with me, just as she had said she would before she passed. Tears rolled down my cheeks, and chills spread through my body. I closed my eyes and imagined Mom standing there with me. I could feel her warmth and comfort, which I had counted on for so many years. Calm filled every inch of my being at a cellular level.

I don't know how long I stood there, as I was a bit disoriented when I opened my eyes. Although the purple butterfly had flown away, my sense of calm remained with me for a while, along with a new feeling of lightness, freedom, and expansion. I smiled from ear to ear as I cherished this heart connection with Mom that transcended heaven and Earth and validated my willingness to be curious and my choice to believe in this symbol. And to think that only one year earlier, I had not believed purple butterflies existed in nature! As I finished my walk, my body felt serene and strong for the first time in several days.

After a week off from work, it was time to return to the office, although nothing there seemed important anymore. I went in each day and sat in meetings, wondering why my team members were so focused on discussing such petty things. No one really knew what to say to me. They would tell me, "You'll feel better soon" and, "Everything will be okay," but how could they really know what would happen next? I could not have predicted the events of the previous three years, so what made them know how I felt? I knew they were well intentioned and just trying to help, but their words made me feel only more detached and out of place. As such, I kept quiet most days, although that was becoming increasingly difficult, as I was the leader of the group and my role required me to make decisions to guide our direction and strategy. Now, there was a void for me in that space. My focus had shifted after I'd said goodbye to my mother. No longer were any strategic juices flowing in my mind, and my passion for solving client problems had dwindled. I knew I needed much more time to heal.

Still, as I reflected on the journey of the past three years, I had a newfound strength inside me, at the core of my being, a voice of my own, which I felt confident in listening to. This voice was screaming loudly at me to put myself first and allow the healing process to continue in its own time. As such, I decided the best option was to transition decision-making authority to my next in line, the number two leader whom I partnered with most days and relied on a great deal. I was not sure how long it would be before I felt comfortable making work decisions. From a financial standpoint, I did know that I needed to keep showing up for work. This seemed like a viable option to meet my conflicting needs. It also gave me the freedom to leave work early some days when the wall of grief crept into my mind and took over every cell of my being.

As the weeks went by, I started to transition to a new normal and to cope from a place of confidence. Surviving two major life transitions in a three-year period represented more trauma than I could fully comprehend, yet it was my reality. I was willing to let go of life as I knew it, and I felt comfortable being raw in my pain and able to talk about it with others. Life was forever changed from my vantage point, in part because of my deepening faith in something greater than myself and in part because of my choice to believe that there was more to life than work. That the boundaries my mind had set were expandable beyond anything I knew to be possible. And that being present and aware in each moment was much more important than knocking out a task on my to-do list.

As I came to trust in my true self and became comfortable in my own skin in a way I never had before, I chose to stop moving through my days on autopilot. From the place I had grown into, the person I had become, I now noticed little things, like tree branches swaying in the breeze as I drove down the street. I believed I had reached the purest sense of authenticity I had ever felt. This heart-opening journey was a result of my choice over time to take off my many masks and find my truest self, and to be willing to live from an authentic place day in and day out.

As I moved through each day trying to find meaning in life and make sense out of the emptiness I felt, my chest still felt as if it were cut open and I continued to struggle to find ways to comfort myself in the midst of this deep grief. I was so grateful for the support I got from many friends during that time. One day, my close friend Cassie offered for me to step away from my daily life and go visit her in Colorado. Before I had said goodbye to my mother, the old me would have declined the invitation, feeling obligated to continue working and taking care of my children and life tasks. Now, instead of saying no, I paused and sat with the vision of what it would feel like to be at the base of the mountains of Colorado Springs—how calming that would feel for my soul. As a smile grew on my face, I said yes to Cassie's offer.

When I arrived, we went for a hike in the mountains. In some ways, I felt as if I were discovering something new with each step. The majestic beauty of the view distracted me enough from my grief that I felt at peace. Here I was, on a trail I had traveled many times before with Cassie, yet this time I experienced it differently, noticing each detail of the trees alongside me as I walked.

Around the next turn, the trail narrowed suddenly. I paused and looked over the edge slightly, seeing the sharp cliff that descended into a deep crevice only a few feet away. The old me would have clung to the inside of the trail and looked down at my footing, not out over the crevice, curious about the view.

When we arrived back at Cassie's house, my grief began to gain traction in my thoughts again. We went inside and sat on the couch, and Cassie said, "Rebecca, I really want to help you heal your pain; I'm just not sure how. What does it feel like inside?"

I responded, "It feels very empty, and I still feel as if I have a deep ravine running through my chest."

She wrapped her arm around my shoulder and started to guide me down a path of remembering all that my mother represented to me. We started with my children. While I felt accomplished in my various work roles, the day I became a mother was quite scary, as I had no clue how to care for a baby. I felt inadequate and somewhat helpless. I was exhausted from thirty hours of labor, followed by cesarean section surgery, when my son was born, and all I wanted to do was sleep. I had no concept of putting someone else first, before my own needs. I was grateful to be in a hospital at that moment and able to focus on my needs while someone else cared for my new bundle of joy.

As I sat there talking to Cassie, I remembered the moment a few days after my son's birth when my mother arrived at the hospital. It was such a relief to me to have her there, giving me help and guidance. When she held my son, she knew just how to comfort and calm him and how to put him to sleep. Like many other things Mom did in her life, she knew what to do in every moment and she did it effortlessly, while never drawing attention to herself.

As Cassie and I talked about my experience of learning how to be a mother, I realized that my mom represented my "owner's manual," my reference point, for each stage of child development from the time each of my children was born—even when I didn't know I needed help. As I reflected on these memories, a section of the black hole in my chest started to feel whole again, and in a way healed. I closed my eyes and sat quietly with this feeling.

Cassie and I continued on this discovery path of all my mother represented to me. After countless hours and memories shared, I started to feel different. I was a little lighter and more comfortable, speechless yet calm. I felt as if I had just completed a process of allowing myself to transition to a place of holding my mom's memory fully in my heart, like she had become a part of me, versus being something I had lost forever. I felt complete again. I was so touched by Cassie's willingness to support me in this way, to facilitate another layer of the healing process for me. I was also grateful for the person I had chosen to become, someone who was willing to push my edges of belief beyond anything my mind could imagine and to allow help in new and different ways.

After this experience, my new normal changed again. It gave me strength to continue the expansion of my authentic journey and to become comfortable with my truest self.

I flew back home two days later, feeling a little more settled and a little stronger. Back at work, demands on my time increased as the consulting practice I had created continued to grow nationally. I was being required more and more to travel to other cities in the United States, meet with clients, and present at conferences. The executives of the company I was working for had noticed my leadership capabilities and the growth of the business I had created. My manager came to me two months later and explained that I was being considered for an executive-level role. She offered several tools to prepare me for such a transition, including access to an executive coach. I now had the benefit of attending more and more senior-level meetings strategizing about the future of the company. I loved my job and the experience I was being offered to sharpen my skills and take on more responsibility. The executive coach helped me with my platform, appearance, and executive-presence skills.

While everything seemed to be exactly what I thought I wanted, something still wasn't quite right. I didn't care for the location of my job. I was increasingly feeling overwhelmed, and when I took a good look at my calendar, I knew why. I had just been away for work for the previous fourteen days, home for only twenty-four hours. When I was in town, I was on work phone calls more and more frequently when I picked up my children from school. When this happened, my daughter's face would turn red with anger and she would tell me to get off the phone. One day, she told me not to pick her up at all if I was going to be on the phone. She told me that she would rather stay and play with her friends at school instead of having me pick her up earlier, under those circumstances.

There she was, speaking up for herself at the age of six, completely confident in her beliefs and not afraid to say what was on her mind. It was quite a wake-up call for me. I had definitely misjudged that situation, and the feeling of my daughter choosing aftercare over spending time with me stuck with me through dinner.

That night, I sat quietly with myself after putting my children to bed. I reflected on the experiences I'd had earlier in the year and knew inside that something needed to change. I thought about the three things I was most passionate about: raising my children, solving client problems, and driving change in healthcare. My number-one priority was getting the leftovers of my time and attention. I decided that being around to raise my children was simply more important than any executive position or any amount of money. While I had survived deep losses of the heart over the previous three years, I had experienced the benefit of seeing firsthand that life can change quickly. I had also strengthened beyond question my belief that my faith would guide me on a path to find an appropriate role in a local company, a place where I could contribute in a meaningful way while still being able to drive home at the end of each day.

I decided it was time to make a change professionally. I took out my notebook and started to write down what I was interested in doing and who I knew to help me. Over the next few days, I was able to connect with several leaders in different companies through the network of people I had developed in Nashville.

Over several months, I explored different options and, with each step, chose to let go of the outcome. I was more focused on making the best choice than I was on making a change. I also was fortunate to have a job while looking for a new one.

While I continued to heal more and more each day, I was still living through the year of "firsts." Christmastime was the toughest, as that was Mom's favorite time of year. I allowed myself the grace of time and space in December to feel the depth of loss in the midst of the celebration of Christ's birth. One day, I found a snow globe at Target with an angel inside it, along with the inscription "may you feel the joy and grace of the season." It made me feel as if Mom was speaking to me and encouraging me to feel happy in spite of my loss.

Shortly after the start of the new year, I received a verbal offer for an executive position in a global healthcare company headquartered in Nashville. I was energized by the mission and found the quality of talent in the company to be similar to that of my current employer. I was excited to go to work with several wicked-smart people who challenged the status quo and had a passion for excellence. It was the right inspiration I needed to refuel my work life.

I resigned from my job in mid-February, a few weeks before my mom's birthday—another one of those big firsts to survive without being able to call or go to Austin to celebrate with her in person. I knew I needed some time off in between jobs to clear the grief that had resurfaced, and my children and I were able to visit Colorado and ski right after my mom's birthday. The mountains and snow provided much-needed peace for my soul.

I started my new job in late March and dove into my new role quickly while learning the nuances of the new company and culture. I felt light in my step again, and my strategic mind ignited quickly around my new areas of focus. My coworkers were welcoming and eager to help me get settled. As Mother's Day approached in May, I was caught by surprise, feeling as if I were wading in quicksand again, unable to move at times, wandering around in a fog. There I was, a mother without a mother, on a day meant to celebrate mothers. My children and I ventured out for our annual tradition of a hike and picnic in the park, and as we walked along the trail, tears poured down my cheeks. Being outside helped me relax and reminded me to be present in the moment and celebrate being a mother myself.

As I approached the anniversary of Mom's passing a few weeks later, I had many different emotions at once. I still felt a little lost without my mother around, but as I reflected on the previous year, I felt grateful to have survived it. I shifted my focus outside myself, as I wanted to celebrate my amazing mother, who had given to me from a bottomless heart of love, willingly and effortlessly.

I sat quietly the night before the anniversary of her death, remembering how I had felt just a year earlier. I closed my eyes and sought guidance from my inner voice, listening for ideas about what would honor Mom the most. I awoke the next day with a surprising feeling of comfort. It was almost as if Mom were walking beside me, showing me how to celebrate her. I went for a hike in the park on a trail we had enjoyed together, I bought and planted a magnolia tree in my backyard, and I put the top down on my convertible and went for a drive while I played her piano music, feeling the wind on my face. I ended the day with friends at Bluebird on the Mountain, an outdoor concert at the Vanderbilt Observatory. As the day came to an end and I lay down to sleep, I was joyous at having been able to honor Mom in a special way while also, amazingly, having survived the anniversary of her passing.

I awoke the next day to a new normal, something that was becoming comfortable each time I felt a shift. I was thriving in my new job and feeling the positive difference of sleeping in my bed every night. I realized that I had lost about ten pounds, not through anything I had done consciously but likely as a result of the reduction in my stress and my increase in restful sleep. There was also a noticeable difference in the way my son and daughter interacted with me. They were less timid and growing more at ease each day. Now that I was choosing a less stressful life and being more physically present for them—able to participate in more school events, whether to hear a performance during the day or cheer from the sidelines of a soccer game—their happiness and gratitude showed in the smiles on their faces.

As I finished my cup of coffee and prepared to embrace a new day, I was grateful for my new normal and the woman I had become.

Epilogue:

Pushing My Edges

*Faith sees the invisible, believes the
incredible, and receives the impossible.*
—Rebecca Munn

It's been ten years since my mother passed. As I reflect
on the person I have become, I am filled with joy and
comfort. I have chosen to accept reality as it is each
day, although that practice is harder some days than
others. And I have incorporated a daily meditation of
gratitude—counting my many blessings and honoring

the unknown, which continues to teach me the richness life has to offer when I least expect it. While I miss my mom's physical presence every day, I have countless stories of encountering purple butterflies along my path, always when I least expect it.

One of the most memorable experiences happened when my children and I ventured to Asheville, North Carolina for a weekend. On our first day, we went for a hike along a trail in the Great Smoky Mountains. As we approached the trailhead, we came upon some bright yellow-and-black butterflies gathered around something on the ground in a pool of water. They grabbed our attention not just because they were stunning in color but also because the water was right in the middle of the trail. In a place that was new to us, these butterflies reminded us to be present on the trail, to be present in the moment, and to pay attention.

As we continued on the path, our hearts and beliefs expanded as we saw a swarm of tiny purple butterflies appear almost out of nowhere. There were at least fifteen or twenty of them flying around, following along with us at knee level while we hiked. Every time we tried to take a picture or a video to capture the moment, the iridescent little treasures barely showed up to the naked eye. We could not see them in the photo, yet we knew they were there. As we shared our hike with these purple butterflies, we felt comfort and joy and a sense of calm. We felt connected to Mom in a special way, believing even more ardently that she was with us.

The other day I went for a walk around Richland Creek, something I do every week with my chocolate Labrador named Coco. I was feeling unsettled in my heart, exhausted from a couple of crazy weeks of school starting and work struggles. As I started on the loop, I paused for a moment and decided to break my pattern of always turning left first. I turned right instead, and as I did so, I became very focused on the trees and flowers, as it seemed liked a brand-new trail for me. I became more connected with and present in my surroundings and explored every turn with wonder, not sure what might be around the next corner. I was completely focused on the moment and aware of my surroundings, and my heart started to settle as the beauty of nature took over my focus.

As I walked along the path, a surprise greeted me: a tiny, iridescent purple butterfly flying above a bush at eye level. When I had tried in the past to watch this type of butterfly, I had never been able to see the color of its outside wings as it landed on something. Every other time, the butterfly had appeared to vanish, until it took flight again.

This day was different. I stopped, closed my eyes, and allowed myself to feel my mother's presence from the inside out, to connect with her on a deeper level than I had achieved since she had passed. Then I opened my eyes. The butterfly landed on a leaf, and as I stood quietly, I could see its outside wings. They were mostly white, with some specs of gray and black. A calm feeling poured through every cell in my body, and I believed that Mom was there with me in that moment, helping me release my struggles and return my focus to what matters most: connections of the heart. And in the process, I was able to see more than I had before.

Several personal experiences recently have reminded me of how precious life can be. While I have carried my new normal forward, I have allowed the busyness of life to take over some days. These personal experiences have helped me connect again at a heart level, whether it was my walking buddy discovering that her husband had cancer, or a lifelong friend losing her mother suddenly in the night, or results from a preventive screening that surprised me. While my test results turned out okay, they caught me off guard at first and gave me enough pause to connect with what is most important. To push my edges of illusion that tomorrow will come just as yesterday passed.

So what is the difference now between the person I was before I went through my divorce and said goodbye to Mom and the person I am today? I am more settled and grounded than ever before, even when Mom was alive. As I reflect on this story in my book and in my life, I know the changes in me have likely come about because of two things: 1) the far-reaching impact Mom had on me by teaching me by example to live each day to the fullest, not to sweat the small stuff, and by showing me by example how to give from a bottomless heart full of love, and 2) my choice to continue my lifelong passion for learning, expand my edges, and believe I am worthy of a continued connection with her spirit. It is that belief that continues to surprise me when I least expect it.

A few months ago, as I walked my chocolate Lab named Coco around Richland Creek, I was reflecting on the many stories I had just heard from my two teenagers about the profound week they had just spent at camp, giving their service and talents to special-needs children, allowing those kids to experience something as close to a normal camp experience as was feasible at Camp Barnabus.

As I turned with the path around a corner, I paused in my thoughts and stared up at the trees to see if I could discern what might be transpiring with a bird that was speaking out loudly, making beautiful sounds as it spoke. When I returned my eyes to the hiking path, there it was—one of those sweet little iridescent purple butterflies, flying across the path from left to right at eye level, as if it wanted to be seen. It warmed my heart and brought a smile to my face. As I processed this surprise and reflected on my children's experiences at camp, I realized that my mom had been a powerful and busy angel with them, working to expand their hearts as they served other children and to remind my precious children how fortunate each of them is.

I have seen many instances of purple butterflies since the first time I spotted one, three days after my mother passed from this physical life, whether on cards in a store, on boxes of Scotties tissues, painted on a cookie in a Starbucks when I stopped in to meet my friend Brad, or on a SpongeBob SquarePants float that my massage therapist saw at Disney World. I am amazed by how I am no longer caught off guard by these experiences, as they represent continued proof of my connection with Mom, which transcends heaven and Earth. These purple butterflies are something I have come to believe will show up when I need them to, either to help me celebrate the many joys of life or to provide support in challenging times.

One such challenge that cut me to my core, yet again, was experiencing the impact of the past two years, watching my teenage son be affected with central-nervous-system damage, a side effect of the HPV vaccine. It has taken almost two years for his body to return to a somewhat normal state, sans some permanent scar tissue in a scary place. And to think his case was mild compared with others I have seen on CNN.

Somehow, I had the strength and courage to put one foot in front of another every day of his ninth-grade year of high school that he missed, every day that the pediatrician refused to admit that he could be experiencing adverse reactions to the vaccine and take action to treat the subsequent damage, every day when my son woke up and crawled to the bathroom because he said his legs wouldn't work, and every day that went by without treatment as the virus caused more damage. I know it was my deep faith and my belief in something bigger than myself, and my authentic connection to my mother's spirit, that gave me courage and strength and kept me going. And here I am, delighted that my son is strong and healthy again, and knowing the symbol of the purple butterfly made a lasting impact on me. These are all more proof points to support my heart-opening expansion to authenticity and confirmation that what we believe is absolutely what we experience.

As I consider how the journey of this book started and how many twists and turns have delayed its completion, I have discovered something interesting—a kind of a parallel meaning between my journey and that of a caterpillar before it becomes a butterfly. As a child, I was a caterpillar, wandering around somewhat in the dark, learning and growing along the way. As fear crept in, I created protection around me, similar to a shield or cocoon. As my journey progressed, I built layers and layers of that protection around me and my heart, deepening the cocoon, each layer representing deep-seated beliefs and presenting a different mask of who I thought I was supposed to be from an outward perspective.

I have chosen to have the courage to allow my heart-opening experiences to transform the life I lead today, to fill each day with expansive joy and a daily practice of gratitude for the person I have become. And now I believe, beyond any shadow of a doubt and with the utmost conviction, that what you believe is what you experience. And once I truly let go of all the layers of my cocoon and set them free, I transformed into a butterfly and now live an authentic life with my heart wide open.

Acknowledgments

 The lovely gift we each have as individuals here on Earth is that we are each purely unique in all aspects of our being. Each of us experience life individually through our own lens and remember experiences in our own ways. Our perspectives and the way we store memories are also unique to each of us.

As I was living through two major life transitions within a three-year time span, I kept a journal and captured my thoughts and feelings along the way. While I started writing this book several times over a nine-year period, I finally broke through my writing walls when I started capturing my story on a blog. All of a sudden, I had readers depending on me to share more. I felt obligated to them to keep going and post new chapters on a regular basis. I would receive comments from total strangers such as: "Wish you would write more! I lost my mom in 2009 after a long illness, and I was touched deeply by your story," and: "Thank you so much for giving me words when I can't find them."

Finishing the story on the blog was rewarding and yet therapeutic at the same time. The unexpected benefit was that it allowed for the continued release of my grief on many more levels. I was delighted to have remained committed to the process of documenting, over a six-month period, the many twists and turns of my life experiences. And I thought I was finished—until I sought input from a professional editor and learned I needed at least double the amount of content, if not triple, for a published book. Two more years later, this is the finished product, or version 1.0—who knows where this journey will lead me?

Many loved ones have supported me through these ups and downs and have encouraged me to share my experiences through this book. I am truly grateful for my support system. My family put up with my trials and tribulations as I progressed in my writing. I thank my father, my four older sisters, and my son and daughter for being supportive and loving as I struggled at times and yet ultimately succeeded in capturing my story, even when the specifics differed from their memories in some ways.

I have received countless hours of support from friends throughout this journey. They have guided me, encouraged my creative process, urged me to keep going, and enabled me to transition into the most authentic self I have ever experienced. Special thanks to Lyn, Cassie, Corinne, Liza, Cindy, Rene, Chuck, Martyn, Stephanie, Clara, Beth, and Jay. I am also grateful for their many gifts of purple butterflies, one of which is included as a photograph in Chapter 10, from my friend Liza's daughter, Raleigh.

One friend in particular supported me in an extra-special way: Karen T. She gave me courage, was a great mentor as an author herself, and was a cheerleader along the way as I published snippets of my story on my blog, ThePurpleButterflyBlog.com. She provided guidance on the nuances of writing a book and on publishing options and how to navigate that process.

I am also very grateful for the guidance and counsel of my editor Annie Tucker, who coached me on developing scenes and characters and worked with me in such a collaborative way as I finalized this manuscript. Through the process, Annie was helpful and thoughtful, recommending the addition of details to bring my story more to life. In addition, Brooke Warner and the She Writes Press team have been a delight to work with and have demystified the publishing process for me, making it possible to bring *The Gift of Goodbye* to people like you. Thank you Brooke and team.

Mostly, I am deeply grateful to my sweet mother, who supported and loved me beyond measure while she was alive. She helped shape the woman I have become and, through life-changing experiences, taught me the power of connecting beyond physical appearances. There is a memorial hopscotch within the Lady Bird Johnson Wildflower Center Family Garden in Austin, TX, that has purple butterflies painted on the hopscotch stepping stones. I am grateful to visit and celebrate Mom when I am in Austin.

About the Author

*T*he *Gift of Goodbye* is a story about my transition from living life from a place of fear to trusting
my faith in something greater than myself, opening my
eyes to a whole new world. The story is my account of
living through two major life transitions within a three-
year span and the resulting shift I made in the process,
due to the lasting gift of love from my now-deceased
mother, my courage, and the choice I made to expand
into more of who I am at my core as everything about

life as I knew it changed. My intention in sharing my story is to provide firsthand examples from my own heart-opening expansion that will encourage you to believe that you, too, can form new beliefs and new connections and elevate your experience to a higher level of authenticity.

Rebecca Whitehead Munn, MBA is a general manager of a healthcare services business for an employee-owned boutique consulting firm. She has a BBA in marketing with a minor in psychology from the University of Texas at Austin and an executive Masters of Business administration degree from the University of Colorado. She leverages her expertise as a certified HBDI professional through all of her interactions to inform expectations and guide communications. In her spare time, she enjoys spending time outdoors with her two teenage children, friends, and chocolate lab, Coco, practicing yoga, snow skiing, golfing, and entertaining. She has lived in Nashville, Tennessee since 2005.

Author photo © Tony Hayes, Verve Studios Photography

Selected Titles from She Writes Press

Don't Leave Yet: How My Mother's Alzheimer's Opened My Heart by Constance Hanstedt. $16.95, 978-1-63152-952-8. The chronicle of Hanstedt's journey toward independence, self-assurance, and connectedness as she cares for her mother, who is rapidly losing her own identity to the early stage of Alzheimer's.

Four Funerals and a Wedding: Resilience in a Time of Grief by Jill Smolowe. $16.95, 978-1-938314-72-8. When journalist Jill Smolowe lost four family members in less than two years, she turned to modern bereavement research for answers—and made some surprising discoveries.

All Set for Black, Thanks: A New Look at Mourning by Miriam Weinstein. $16.95, 978-1-63152-109-6. A wry, irreverent take on how we mourn, how we remember, and how we keep our dead with us even as we (sort of) let them go.

Rethinking Possible: A Memoir of Resilience by Rebecca Faye Smith Galli. $16.95, 978-1-63152-220-8. After her brother's devastatingly young death tears her world apart, Becky Galli embarks upon a quest to recreate the sense of family she's lost—and learns about about healing and the transformational power of love over loss along the way.

Falling Together: How to Find Balance, Joy, and Meaningful Change When Your Life Seems to be Falling Apart by Donna Cardillo. $16.95, 978-1-63152-077-8. A funny, big-hearted self-help memoir that tackles divorce, caregiving, burnout, major illness, fears, and low self-esteem—and explores the renewal that comes when we are able to meet these challenges with courage.

The Space Between: A Memoir of Mother-Daughter Love at the End of Life by Virginia A. Simpson. $16.95, 978-1-63152-049-5. When a life-threatening illness makes it necessary for Virginia Simpson's mother, Ruth, to come live with her, Simpson struggles to heal their relationship before Ruth dies.